THE UNIFORMS OF TRAFALGAR

Although there have been many accounts of the battle of Trafalgar, biographies of the great Nelson himself and descriptions of life in the navy at that time there has not, until this book, been a survey of the uniforms worn by officers and men in the three combatant navies – Britain, France and Spain.

John Fabb and Jack Cassin-Scott first set the uniforms in the context of life aboard a fighting ship during the Napoleonic wars – a severely disciplined, often brutal existence punctuated by battles, like Trafalgar, of terrifying bloodiness.

They go on to describe the uniforms, rank by rank and nation by nation, from the splendour of the admiral in full dress, through each rank in full dress and undress versions until, at the bottom of the scale, we find the starkly functional clothing of the ordinary seaman.

Particular care has been taken to present uniforms from original sources and Dress Regulations and, where appropriate, to show back views – so often neglected yet of much interest to, for example, modellers. In addition there is information on swords and decorations. In all cases the illustrations have been taken from contemporary sources.

John Fabb and Jack Cassin-Scott have both been involved in military costume history for many years. Among their many publications are *Victorian and Edwardian Navy from old photographs*, *Victorian and Edwardian Army from old photographs* and *Uniforms of the Napoleonic Era*.

96 pages   4 colour plates   89 black and white photographs

Also of interest

A DICTIONARY OF MILITARY UNIFORM
W. Y. Carman, FSA, FRHistS   *168 pages, 188 illustrations, 9 colour plates*

BATTLE OF TRAFALGAR
Geoffrey Bennett   *224 pages, 23 diagrams, 16 photographs*

COLLECTING OLD TOY SOLDIERS
Ian McKenzie   *160 pages, 12 colour and 65 black and white photographs*

VICTORIAN AND EDWARDIAN NAVY FROM OLD PHOTOGRAPHS
A. P. McGowan and John Fabb   *120 pages, 172 photographs*

VICTORIAN AND EDWARDIAN ARMY FROM OLD PHOTOGRAPHS
W. Y. Carman and John Fabb   *128 pages, 154 photographs*

The Uniforms

JOHN FABB and

# of Trafalgar

JACK CASSIN–SCOTT

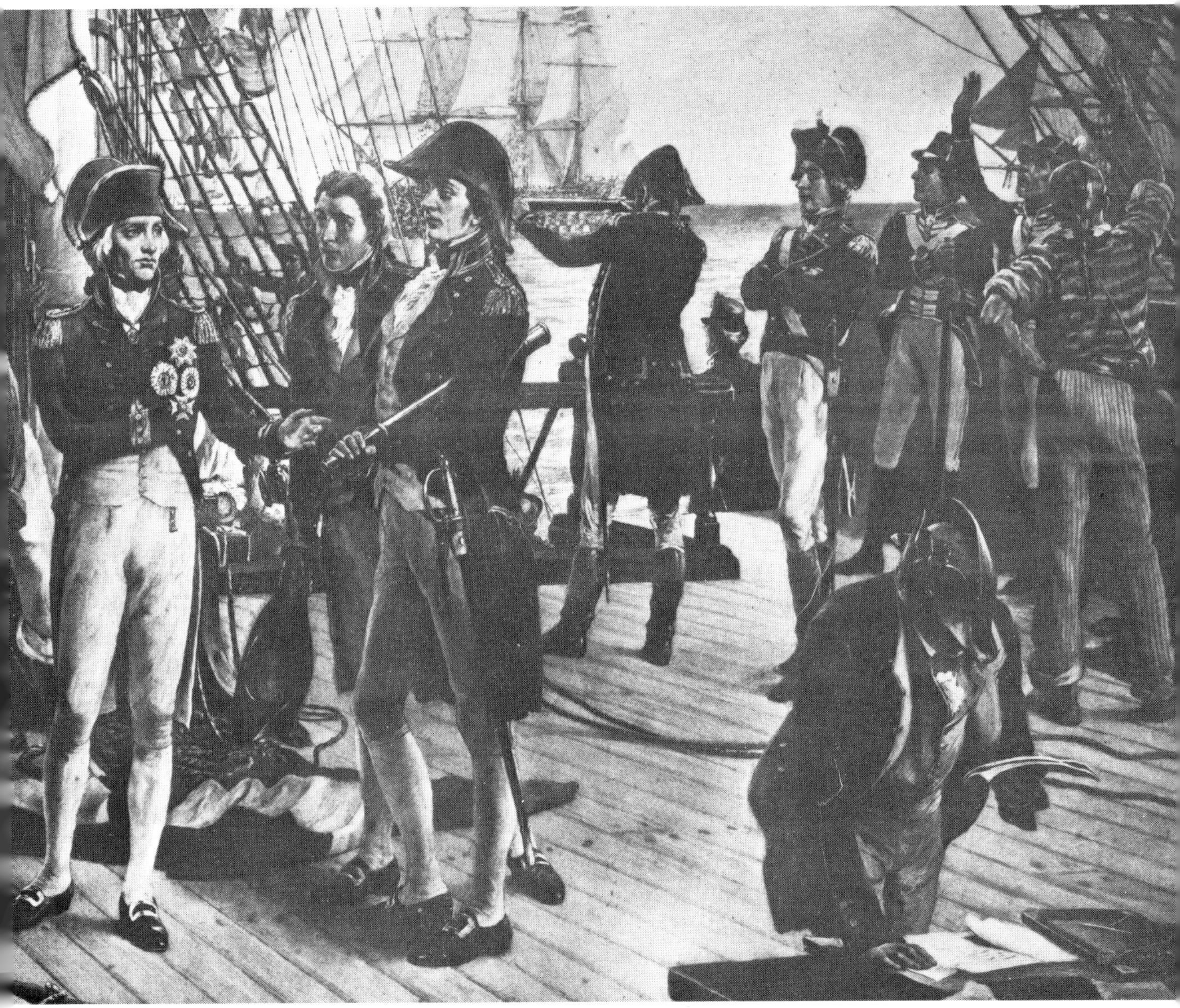

Hippocrene Books Inc.
New York

First published 1977

HIPPOCRENE BOOKS, INC.
171 Madison Avenue, New York, N.Y. 10016

Library of Congress Catalog Card Number 76-55138
ISBN 0 88254 432 2

Printed in Great Britain

Contents

Acknowledgments 6
Introduction 7

Life at Sea 11
The British Navy 16
The French Navy 42
The Spanish Navy 72

Glossary 81
Appendix A: *Naval outfitters, hatters and button manufacturers, 1805* 93
Bibliography 95
Index 96

Acknowledgments

Our grateful thanks for their great help and assistance for all the information and photographs provided, to Monsieur H. Cras and staff of the Musée de la Marine, Paris, France (Pls 5, 40–68, 71–3); Signor Laureano Carbonell of the Museo Maritimo, Barcelona, Spain (Pls 79, 80); Signor Roberto Barreiro-Meiro of the Museo Naval, Madrid, Spain (Pls 74–8), and the National Maritime Museum, Greenwich, England (Pls 1–4, 6–12, 14–16, 18–24, 27–32, 35–9, 69, 70, 84–8) for the generous advice and photographic assistance. Plates 17, 25, 26, 33, 34, 81–3 are from the Author's collection.

Our thanks also to Charles Worvill for translations from the French and to Jack Blake for photographing various items of uniform.

1 Meeting of Nelson and his Captains on the eve of Trafalgar

Introduction

In recent years there has been an increased interest in naval and military history. Practically all the facets of these subjects have been discussed in a variety of publications from newspapers and magazines of the Services, to the general reader interest displayed in popular magazines. Television and films have played their part and made the public more aware of the diversified types of uniform and perhaps made them wish to enquire more deeply into the subject. Detailed studies have been made and published on campaigns, tactics and logistics. There has also developed an upsurge of interest in the uniforms and equipment of these forces. Uniforms have become a highly specialized subject and with regard to the armies of the world the volume of literature has increased considerably in the last four years.

Every army and practically every regiment and corps has been the subject of close scrutiny but the navies of the world have not received this detailed study; certainly, the uniforms and the number of books published in the last 50 years is extremely small with many navies receiving only a passing reference in a volume devoted to the complete armed forces of a nation. Only in the United States of America have there been books on a large scale devoted to the dress and accoutrements of the sea services. This book is not a history of the navy and does not discuss the battle of Trafalgar from a tactical or political point of view. It devotes itself, instead, to one period of naval dress history, and covers the uniforms of all three belligerents at a time of great changes for these countries.

The naval dress of the Napoleonic era had little of the glamour attached to the other military uniforms of that time. The leaders of the three nations involved had little interest in the sartorial elegance of their sea forces and contented themselves with their armies, which could be seen on a much larger scale and as a whole presenting a much better display of their power.

The close quarters of a ship at sea made it impractical to wear the plumes, belts and pelisses that had begun to appear in the dress of the land forces, and even epaulettes, which were the distinctive mark of an officer, had a difficult passage before becoming part of a commissioned officer's wardrobe. The naval uniform was in fact the most practical of its time and was similar to civilian dress of the period. Blue was universally chosen by the navies as the basic colour of their arm, presumably because it is associated with the sea and is a colour which will not noticably fade.

The naval uniform worn by the British navy was first authorized in 1748. Prior to this date naval officers tended to indulge their own whim or follow the army. The Duke of Bedford, who was First Lord at the time, had received various proposals for a uniform based on the royal livery of red, blue and gold.

The Duke, however, replied to these officers that, 'The King has determined otherwise, for, having seen my Duchess riding in the park a few days ago in a habit of blue faced with white, the dress took the fancy of his Majesty, who appointed it for the uniform of the Royal Navy.' This anecdote is probably apocryphal, however, as the King had already seen similar models based on these colours, though the sight of the Duchess of Bedford may have decided the matter. The Duke of Bedford's family has, in fact, a bill for a blue and white riding habit which may be the one mentioned in the story.

In the April of 1748 orders were issued for the first time regarding the naval officer's dress. Until 1857 only officers were provided with a regulation for uniform. Seamen wore clothing sold to them by the purser or made out of material issued from his stores; by bulk buying a certain uniformity could be attained by the lower deck men.

After 1748 the uniform was altered in 1767, 1774 and again in 1783. New uniforms were authorized in 1787 which were still in use at the time of Trafalgar.

The French navy which had recovered much of its power and lustre in the American War of Independence, was neglected by Napoleon, the new ruler of France. He was a military tactician and had little interest in the navy other than as a means of conveying his army from one point to another. Trafalgar proved

2 Signals being hoisted and flown at Trafalgar

3 Guncrew cleaning out the gun after firing (after Thomas Stothard)

to be the end of French expansion in the West Indies and of an invasion of England, the armies were withdrawn for a land invasion of Prussia and Austria and many French sailors and marines were put to war in the field as part of the army.

With the Revolution in France the old uniforms had been swept away and new regulations were drawn up for a new sea service. This was to be the most modern dress regulation in Europe at that time, whereas the British and the Spanish fashions were still firmly planted in the eighteenth century with only a few innovations, such as epaulettes. Indeed the Spanish navy did not adopt these items until much later.

The French sailors were dressed in much the same fashion as their British counterparts: shirts, trousers and sometimes a blue jacket, shoes worn only in port or on parade. The tricolour cockade was often the only uniform item for crew members. The officers were regulated in detail for their uniforms as much as their adversaries and were dressed in a similar manner to the army.

Nearly every country in Europe wore at least a version of French uniform. Most significantly, the first years of the nineteenth century saw the abolition of powdered hair and queues (pigtails) and the new fashion of short, natural hair which was an innovation brought about by the French Revolution. The white of the Bourbons and the lily crest were replaced at first by the phyrgian cap of the Revolution, resting upon an anchor, but this was later removed and the Imperial crown of Napoleon adopted. Red and white had been the colours of the French navy before the Revolution and these were maintained all through the Napoleonic wars.

The French navy lost many of its officers because of the political upheaval and the replacements had not the ability that had been displayed by Admiral

Suffren in the late 1780s and the sea battles of the American Revolution where British dominance at sea came under question. The 'Glorious First of June' was the first sea battle of the French Revolution and ended in defeat for the Republic. The battle of the Nile in Aboukir Bay destroyed the French fleet and culminated in the battle of Trafalgar where French naval power was utterly destroyed for the remainder of the Napoleonic era.

Service as an officer in the French navy had been before the Revolution one of the most acceptable aristocratic professions but, since then, the navy had been democratized. All the admirals and practically all the officers had been arrested and flung into prison, or forced to leave the country. On board the ships the cry of 'liberté, fraternité, egalité' announced the end of the old discipline and order.

In the place of seasoned professional officers came men whose single-minded devotion to the Revolution far outweighed their professional capabilities as fighting seamen. The most junior midshipmen and lieutenants with the correct political leanings and captains of small obscure merchant ships became captains of the largest battleships overnight. Seamen were also raised to the rank of officer if their politics were of the right colour. Discipline had disappeared and any attempt to re-introduce it caused meetings of revolutionary councils and denouncement of the officer as a traitor of the people.

Napoleon, once he had restored law and order realized the navy was in a poor condition and some of the original naval officers were induced to return and fight for France, but they were not of the old school and were unable to pull together a navy comparable to that of the British Royal Navy. The names of the ships were destroyed and removed after centuries of use, old emblems discarded – the *esprit de corps* eroded. The new French navy was put to test at Aboukir Bay where the defeat destroyed any morale that had been instilled by the new order. Over 7000 men had been killed or wounded and the French army in Egypt isolated. It was a great blow to morale and also a grievous loss of the skilled men who had been killed or were no longer able to go to sea because of their wounds: a catastrophe from which the navy never recovered.

Life at sea

Once on board a British ship the men were examined to see if they 'Have any hurts or diseases which may render them unfit for service in His Majesty's Navy' – if they had two arms and two legs this was often good enough no matter what other deficiencies might be found.

Once a man was onboard a ship-of-the-line he never knew when he might set foot on shore again. It could be up to five or ten years before he was paid off. His pay was up to 22 shillings and sixpence per month, less deductions for tobacco and clothing. Unfortunately they were often paid with tickets instead of cash and these were difficult to dispose of, and usually meant the men ended up with half their value from a money lender.

When the crew were mustered the first lieutenant would allocate the men to their stations, which were many and needed continuous manning on a warship. The largest group were the landsmen and unskilled hands who had not been to sea before, they were called 'waisters' because they were stationed in the waist of the ship, they kept this area clean and tidy and handled the main and fore sheets. They also looked after the livestock such as pigs, sheep and hens. Manning the bilge pumps was another task for this section.

The 'idlers' worked in the day but not at all at night. This group consisted of the painters, coopers (who repaired and made the casks); the barber who dressed the men's pig-tails and attended the officers' hair also; the butchers who slaughtered the livestock, and the 'captain of the head', an important title for the man who looked after the lavatories at the head of the ship.

The 'after guard' were a group chosen to work the ropes which hauled the yards round to trim the sails, and also the spanker, mainsail and lower staysail. When in action they worked the guns in the after part of the ship and also kept this area clean and tidy.

The older and more experienced seamen were stationed on the fo'c'sle to work the anchor, bowsprit and fore yards. They were the most reliable men in the ship and were called 'sheet anchor men'.

The topmen had the most dangerous job of all and were chosen from amongst the active and young. They worked the sails above the lower yards where one slip could mean death on the deck or sea far below. This group was divided into three sections, one for each mast. A ship's smartness depended on how quickly her topmen could set, furl or reef the sails and scramble down to the decks again. They were hurried along by a length of knotted rope wielded by the bosun's mate. In some ships the captain would flog the last man down, which was always an effective incentive. The seamen were, in time of peace, recruited only for the period of the ship's commission, but in time of war were taken by the press-gangs from the streets of British ports or from the jails.

Savage encounters between the press-gangs and men who resisted impressment were far from uncommon. In the course of the American War of Independence American prisoners taken on board British ships and there were also vessels in which nearly the whole crew was composed of Irishmen who could scarcely speak one word of English. To prevent the hatching of mutinies orders were frequently given and enforced that no conversation in Irish should be allowed on board. The seamen of the fleet deserted at every turn; they were often rough, brutal and drunken and to hold them down was a matter of no small difficulty.

The code of rules governing the Navy, or 'the Articles of War', were therefore of extraordinary severity. Almost any offence could be punished by a court-martial carrying the death penalty. Disobeying orders, hanging back in action, not assisting friends, refusing service because wages had not been paid – a state of things only too common in the navy at that date – deserting, uttering mutinous words, striking a superior officer, neglect in steering a ship, sleeping on watch, and robbery were all punishable by death. The alternative was scouring on the bare back with the cat-of-nine-tails – a terrible implement of torture. Any captain could order 48 lashes without a court-martial. A man could get two dozen for saying that it was not his watch. There are instances when men were flogged for losing a cap or being a minute late in getting down their hammocks. 'Let us do what we will we can gain no goodwill nor satisfaction from our captain, nothing but flogging from morning to night,' the men complained to an admiral, and were flogged round the fleet, entailing a punishment of 500 lashes, for making such a complaint.

Offenders were put into a launch fitted with a platform and shears, to which the men were triced up. The boat was then towed alongside the first ship and a certain number of lashes inflicted, after which the prisoners were allowed to sit down, and their shoulders covered with a blanket, whilst being towed to the next vessel. The wounds had time to close, the blood to congeal, which added to the pain of the torture. The cat was made of nine hempen cords attached to a stout handle, and each cord near the end of the lash was bound with fine twine. After a few lashes it drew blood and the man who had suffered 200, 300, or 500 lashes, if he survived, was completely broken in health and spirits. Though more lashes were given in the army, the cat used was not so formidable and the wounds inflicted much less severe. Besides this, flogging in the army was conducted by the drummers who were generally smaller and weaker men, whereas flogging in the navy was conducted by the boatswain's mates, who were invariably the biggest and most powerful men in the ship. Added to which, they were drilled to flog at periodic intervals, having to belabour a cask under the superintendence of the boatswain.

Besides the floggings by his captain, the seaman often had to undergo much brutality at the hands of his comrades and of the boatswain and his mates. There is record of a case in which a man had his hair burnt off and one ear cut off; an attempt made to hang him by fastening a rope round his neck and hauling him up to a beam; and finally the head clew of his hammock repeatedly cut down, with the result that he fell violently on the deck. The boatswains and the midshipmen carried rattan canes as thick as the little finger with which they beat those men who were slack in performing duty. In the same 'Court Martials' is recorded the case of a man who was flogged to death by the boatswain, and yet the seamen dared not make any complaint. The lieutenant of the watch, when told what had happened, only answered that he was not a judge and the body was hastily thrown overboard.

The food in the navies of the period was little better. Indifferent salt meat,

4 Dancing aboard ship with female companions, which was allowed during this period (after Thomas Stothard)

pease-pudding, and sour beer, salt meat, rancid butter, and 'purser's' cheese – which was generally a stinking compound – with, of course, a good allowance of grog for all. In those days the men received a gill of rum a day, half at the midday meal and half in the evening after 'night-quarters' (which was generally served raw). The weight of food was invariably short – a great and shameful grievance. Beer was issued freely to the men to prevent scurvy. A cask would be broached in the afternoon on deck and the men would come and take it away to drink. On such occasions disorder was very common.

Water was carried in casks, not distilled, and would often be contaminated. The biscuit supplied was so full of weevils that there was a standing service joke about weevils being the only fresh meat tasted once the ship had put to sea. It was not an unknown thing for three seamen to be put on one man's allowance when food ran short.

The food for the crew was divided into messes consisting of eight men in a ship the size of HMS *Victory*. Each mess sat at its own table slung from the deck head between two of the guns. The table itself was kept hooked up between the beams when not in use. Each mess would select a cook from among its own men to collect their provisions from the purser and take them along to the ship's cook in the galley, where they would be cooked in water that was often stagnant. The men drank beer while it lasted because the water was usually bad after a few weeks at sea. They were entitled to a gallon of beer a day and when this was no longer available, a half pint of brandy or rum and sometimes wine. The white wine favoured by British sailors was 'Spanish Mistela', known as 'Miss Taylor'.

On paper the food ration was adequate, but much of it was poor quality and bad. The meals were set out in a weekly pattern: Sunday and Thursday, pork; Tuesday and Saturday, salt beef. The meat would have been salted a long time, even years. The sailors were able to carve boxes and fancy items out of the meat which was 'stoney hard, glistening with salt, dark, gristly and shrunken. Half a sailor's ration of meat was fat and gristle with much bone.' Oatmeal was issued and was called 'Skillagolee' or 'Burgoo', but this also was nauseating. A favourite with the crew was pea soup issued with the salt pork on Sunday or Thursday. Another favourite for those with strong stomachs was to cook the biscuits in the oven to kill the weevils, and then boil it in water with sugar, thus producing a sticky mess called 'Scottish Coffee'. Cheese and butter were included in thr weekly ration as was vinegar.

The crew was allocated tasks by numbers from one to 570, depending on the size of the ship. These numbers were put on the ship's general quarters watch and station bill. The sailor could tell by his number which part of the ship he worked in and also, when action stations were called, the gun crew he worked with and at what task. He had to remember which station he should be at when sailing the ship or during combat, for failure would mean a cuff with the bo'sun's rope end.

The ship's day would start at midnight with the larboard watch being roused by the bo'sun's mates. The men would have to move quickly to avoid the ropes end as they fell out of their hammocks. They slept in their clothes to avoid having to waste time dressing; this would be customary except in the tropics. The previous watch could then snatch a rest for four hours. At 4.00 am

5 Crew of the French privateer *Hasard* (*c.* 1805)

the starboard watch would be called to the deck by the bo'sun's mates to clear the ship's decks. They would have to rig up the pump for sea water and start scrubbing and using pieces of holystone known as 'prayer books'. The deck would be wetted and then, with sand sprinkled over it, those sailors with the holystones would start scouring the sand into the deck until it was clean. The scrubbers would follow, with the swabbers following up to dry the decks. The brass and metalwork of the ship would be cleaned with brick dust and polishing cloths. These men would work to windward of the holystone crew so that the dust would not ruin their efforts. At daylight a sailor would be sent aloft as a look-out, the ship was of course quite blind at night and depended completely on the navigating officer's skill not to hazard the ship. The next task was to stow the hammocks. Each man would lash his hammock with the straw mattress inside together with a blanket, all held by seven regulation turns of a lanyard. These hammocks would then be taken on deck, the men dispersing to their respective divisions. They would stow their hammocks in the netting which surrounded the upper deck of the ship with long strips of canvas placed over them to protect the bedding from the weather. The reason for bringing them on deck was to use them as a protective shield against bullets and grapeshot when in action. The cook would have been roused at 4.00 am to work on the first meal of the day, which was served at 8.00 am, to the pipe call of 'hands to breakfast'. This meal would be eaten at the tables slung between the guns, having been collected by the mess cook. The men were then free until 8.30 am. Further cleaning and polishing would be called for until divisions were sounded at 9.30 am on weekdays and at 10.00 am on Sundays. The captain would inspect the men and marines and go round the whole ship looking for a spot of dirt, dust or grease. White gloves with which to detect dirt were worn, as was customary in the army, but not all captains went to these lengths. The Royal Marines would have also been up at an early hour cleaning their white equipment, polishing buttons and weapons. They were kept separate from the crew, acting as a buffer between authority and the seamen.

They were drilled by their NCO's and practised musketry out to sea. At 12.00 noon the midday meal was served and the watch not at work was allowed to rest. Cards were forbidden but were of course played in some quiet spot with the rum ration to gamble with. This issue at noon would be one gill of pure rum mixed with three gills of water. Debts were paid in rum, because money was usually not available and the paper chits issued were of dubious value anyway. At an hour before dusk, approximately 5.00 pm, the hands would be piped to supper, the third and last meal of the day, consisting of cheese and biscuits and a second ration of rum and beer. At 5.30 pm the Royal Marine drummers would beat to quarters and the men would rush to man the guns. There would then be an inspection by the officers of the crew at gun drill and in some ships officers would reward gun crews with money for skill in loading and re-loading the guns in a fast time – 'three in five', that is three times in five minutes. At 8.00 pm 'down hammocks' would be piped and the men would be allowed to retrieve their bedding and get down below decks to sling them before 'lights out' was piped at 8.10 pm. The lookout was called down from the mast and the ship was then watched from the deck until first light the next day.

On Sundays the daily routine was altered slightly: after the captain's inspection at divisions, the crew would be collected to the quarter deck for divine service followed by the fiddler playing a lively tune while the master's mate got ready to issue the rum ration.

The British Navy

Flag Officers 1795–1812. Full dress

Flag officers, captains and commanders were given a new full dress uniform and epaulettes in the regulations of 1 June 1795. These were in force during the period of 1805, and remained unaltered until March 1812. The new regulations were published in the *London Gazette* over several issues.

The coat was to be of navy-blue cloth as previously worn but with blue facings replacing white. The standing blue collar was edged all round in vellum and check-pattern gold lace. The turnback lapels were also of blue cloth and edged with a gold lace of the same width as the collar. The nine button holes were edged in the same pattern lace. In the Welch and Stalker

6 Sir Thomas Troubridge in admiral's uniform with the Order of St Ferdinand. He was lost at sea in HMS *Blenheim* in 1807 (by Sir William Beechey, RA)

pattern book now in the library of the Victoria and Albert Museum, London, it is noted that 'some officers have their lapels as low as the waist; there being no particular order about that, it being regulated by the will of the wearer; if very fashionable to be as the pattern illustrated in the pattern book.'

The round cuffs were ornamented with gold lace. Admirals were to have three rows of distinction lace around the cuff. Three rows of vertical lace were adorned with a gilt button on the upper edge. The slits were edged with gold lace as were the pockets. These had three buttons which were discernable just under the flap of the pockets, which were decorated with three false button holes edged in gold lace.

Epaulettes were introduced in the 1795 regulations. These had been unofficially worn for some years in the Royal Navy. Twelve years previously Nelson had written very caustically regarding officers wearing them. Calling them 'coxcombs' and 'holding them a little cheap for putting on part of a Frenchman's uniform'. They had been worn in the Marines for at least 20 years previously, and also in the British army by regulars and Militia. The Royal Navy had adopted them because of the failure of foreign troops to recognize them as officers without epaulettes, and in consequence failing to salute them. The epaulettes had a plain gold lace strap (the part resting on the shoulder), with a row of 20 bullions (the fringe hanging down at the end). To denote rank, silver embroidered stars were used, made with silver sequins. The admirals wore two epaulettes, each having three of these stars; vice admirals had two stars and rear admirals one star on each epaulette. The epaulette was also fitted with a gilt brass button at the end nearest the shoulder. A new button

7 (*Below left*) Nelson in the full dress uniform of a rear admiral (*c.* 1805), after Hoppner

8 (*Below*) Sir John Jervis (Earl of St Vincent) in an admiral's full dress uniform with the Order of the Bath (by Sir William Beechey, RA)

9 Nelson wearing the famous 'Chilingk' or plume of triumph, presented to him by the Sultan of Turkey. It had 13 rays which represented the 13 prizes he took at the Battle of the Nile. He is dressed in the full dress uniform of a vice admiral (by L. Guzzardi)

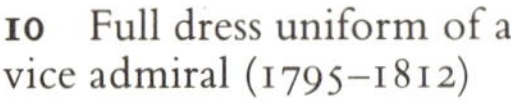

10 Full dress uniform of a vice admiral (1795–1812)

was introduced for flag officers in 1787 and remained unchanged until 1812. This design consisted of a fouled anchor within a beaded circle surrounded by a laurel wreath tied with a bow and set at a slight angle – a design which has remained practically unaltered up to the present day and is still in use.

With this uniform was worn a white waistcoat together with white breeches, stockings and black brass-buckled shoes. Also for the first time the regulations of 1795 mention hats. Flag officers wore gold laced hats in both full dress and undress. It was at this period that the hat, which had been cocked on three sides, became cocked on two, thus altering the whole presentation of the headdress. The back flap was increased in height and the front became straighter after about 1800. Gold bullion fringed tassels were worn by admirals at each end. The front flap of the hat was ornamented with a gold lace strap with a button at one end, and at the other, on the top edge of the hat a black

11 Lord Collingwood in vice admiral's uniform (after Charles Turner)

12 In the full dress uniform of a vice admiral, Lord Cuthbert Collingwood (after Charles Turner)

13 A waxwork effigy of Nelson at Westminster Abbey. Dressed in the full dress uniform of a vice admiral with Orders.

14 Nelson as Rear Admiral of the Blue, aged 39 (by L.F. Abbot)

cockade. Originally worn athwartships by all ranks of officer it became the prerogative of flag officers, the others wearing the hat fore-and-aft (and at the end of the Napoleonic era flag officers were also adopting this method).

On the left breast, it was the custom to have embroidered the stars of the orders of chivalry awarded to admirals in place of the actual orders which were of course made in silver or silver gilt with enamel work.

On board HMS *Victory* Lord Nelson usually wore his undress uniform. Lieutenant Rivers, who served in the *Victory*, described the Admiral as he appeared at the time of Trafalgar:

> His dress was the same as he usually wore, a plain cocked hat with a green shade fixed to it inclining over his right eye but worn nearly square. White neckerchief, white marsalla waistcoat, uniform coat with four stars, casimir breeches, stockings thread and silk mixed, shoes with buckles. His Lordship never altered his dress the three years in the *Victory*; upon two occasions he put on boots for a few hours, when wet.

15 Admiral Sir Edward Pellew, Lord Exmouth in full dress coat (by J. Northcoate)

16 Vice admiral's epaulettes (1795–1812) worn by Nelson

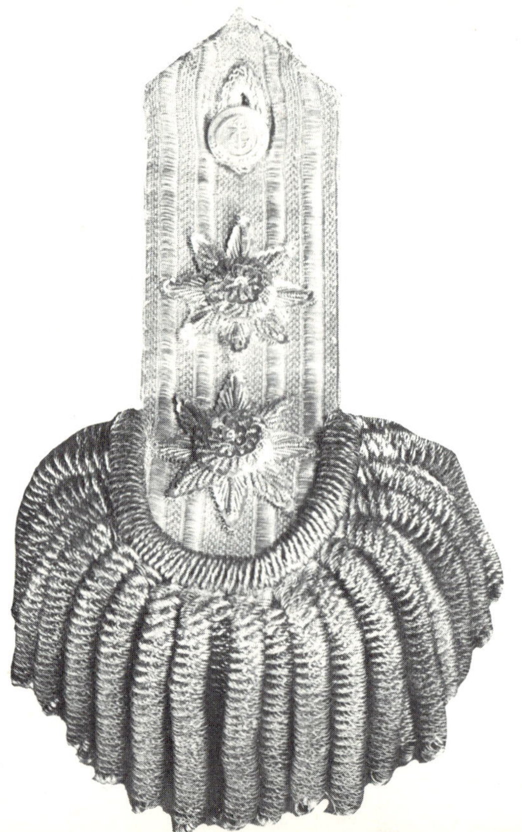

Flag Officers 1795–1812. Undress

The undress uniform for admirals was introduced in 1795 of plain navy-blue cloth cut in the same manner as the full dress coat. The turn-back lapels were without ornamentation except for the buttons, the holes for which were plain. The standing collar was without lace and worn open to display the neck cloth and cravat. The pocket flaps were three pointed, with three gilt buttons underneath. The sleeves were decorated with the appropriate number of gold lace rings, with three gilt buttons on the upper section. The epaulettes were of the same pattern as those worn with the full dress coat and flag officers were to wear them in both orders of dress. The cocked hat was also that worn in the full dress order. Illustration 17 shows the undress uniform of a vice-admiral worn by Lord Nelson at the battle of Trafalgar. It was in this coat he received the fatal bullet wound through the left shoulder, travelling downwards through the chest to the backbone. On the left breast are sewn the embroidered stars of his four orders of chivalry. These were the Order of the Bath at the top, then the Sicilian order of St Ferdinand and Merit, the Turkish order of the Crescent, bestowed by the Sultan of Turkey after the victory at Aboukir; and at the bottom the equestrian order of St Joachem of Leiningen. With this

17 Undress uniform coat of Vice Admiral Nelson without epaulettes (*c.* 1805). The four Orders are: top, Bath; the Crescent; St Ferdinand and St Joachim

(Opposite) Centre figure of a vice admiral in the undress uniform of 1795–1812. This is the figure of Nelson who wore a green eyeshade, shown here turned back. To the left is a warrant officer in the uniform of 1787–1807 with a speaking trumpet. To the right side a captain in the undress uniform of 1797–1812, of three years post. In the background centre is a Royal marine in the uniform of *c.* 1805 (2,600 Royal Marines were present in the Fleet at Trafalgar.) In the background on the right is a seaman in the nondescript uniform worn at Trafalgar.

uniform was worn the white waistcoat and knee breeches as worn for full dress.

The sword worn in the order of dress was the same as full dress. At Trafalgar Lord Nelson was unarmed, his sword remained lying on his cabin table throughout the battle.

When HMS *Victory* reached England after the battle, all Lord Nelson's personal belongings were sent to Lady Hamilton at Merton Park, Surrey. These included the undress uniform Lord Nelson wore at the battle. When Lady Hamilton's financial position became intolerable she sold these relics to Alderman Joshua Smith of the City of London, to whom she owed a considerable sum. The Alderman's widow discovered these items in 1844, packed away in a crate. She sold his coat and waistcoat to Sir Nicholas Harris Nicholas for £150. Subsequently they passed into the hands of Prince Albert, who presented them to Greenwich Hospital. The coat together with four others belonging to Lord Nelson are now in the National Maritime Museum.

Captain 1795–1812. Full dress

The new order of the 1 June 1795 drastically altered the captain's uniform. The white lapels and cuffs which had been a feature of the Royal Navy uniform since 1748 were abolished. The standing collar was of blue cloth edged all round with gold lace and the turnback blue lapels had square ends edged in a gold lace and fitted with nine buttons to each side. These were of gilt brass with a roped edge, within an oval rope design appeared a fouled anchor. This pattern remained in use until 1812 when a crown was added. It was fashionable to wear the lapels buttoned over, except for the top three or four, and no doubt at sea this was more desirable in breezy or inclement weather.

The sleeves were slashed (these had been abolished in 1747 but were now restored) with two rows of lace around the cuff for captains and the slash was edged in two rows of gold lace. Three gilt buttons the same size as those on the lapels were placed on the slashed cuff. The tails of the coat were edged all

18 Rear Admiral Sir Henry Blackwood (by Hoppner)

JACK CASSIN-SCOTT

19 Captain's full dress uniform (1795–1812)

round in a gold lace, the same width lace used on all parts of the coat. Captains of under three years post were to wear only one shoulder epaulette, Senior captains were to have two. These were of the same pattern as flag officers but had plain straps. White waistcoats were worn with this order of dress and white breeches with stockings. By 1805 officers were wearing their cocked hats 'fore-and-aft' only flag officers keeping the old fashioned 'athwartships' until about 1820. The hat was bound in gold lace with a decoration of narrow gold lace with a button to secure the black silk cockade. At each end of the hat was a gold bullion tassel. Many officers disregarded dress regulations and orders were frequently issued to coerce these gentlemen into a uniform recognized by authority. Admiral Earl St Vincent issued an order on 4 November 1797:

> The Commander in Chief having seen several officers of the Fleet on shore, dressed like shop keepers in coloured cloths, and others wearing round hats with their uniforms in violation of the late order of the Right Honourable the Lords Commissioners of the Admiralty, does positively direct that any officer offending against this wholesome and necessary regulation in future, is put under arrest and reported to the Admiral, and let the sentence of a courts martial, such offenders so offending, be what it may, that he never is permitted to go onshore while under the command of the Earl of St Vincent.

(Opposite) A lieutenant of a man-of-war, with speaking trumpet of the Revolutionary Navy, in the uniform of *c.* 1793. A captain in the uniform of *c.* 1802. A quartermaster in the uniform of *c.* 1805

Captain 1795–1812. Undress

The undress coat for captains of over three years post was of plain navy-blue cloth with a stand-and-fall collar, this was without ornament of lace and the lapels with eight brass buttons could be fastened across or left open as in the full dress coat. The lapels were also without lace. This coat did not have the slashed cuffs as in full dress and they had a false round cuff ornamented with three brass buttons and button holes. The pockets on the coat were plain but had the three-button decoration as did the full dress coat. With this uniform epaulettes were optional for captains, and were attached to the coat by passing the straps through a piece of lace sewn to the shoulder, this can be clearly seen in illustration 21. The sword was carried in a black leather sword belt which had lion's head buckles and a snake fastener all in gilt brass. This is the uniform that was usually worn in battle and at sea on other informal occasions. It was completed by a white waistcoat and white breeches and some officers adopted black hessian boots in place of shoes and stockings.

21 *(Below right)* Undress uniform of a captain (1795–1812)

20 *(Below)* Captain with three years seniority (1795–1812) in undress uniform and Hessian boots

22 Lord Cochrane in the undress uniform of a captain

Lieutenant 1787–1812. Full dress

The lieutenants were next in command after the captain. A ship of the line, such as the *Victory* carried as many as eight lieutenants, while smaller ships had one or more. The first lieutenant was responsible for the operation of the ship and was also an executive officer. The second lieutenant was generally in charge of gunnery. November of 1787 saw the reintroduction of full dress uniform for lieutenants after an interval of 20 years. Previously they had only possessed one all-purpose uniform.

The coat was of navy-blue cloth with a standing collar of blue, decorated with a gilt brass button and button hole on each side. The turnback lapels were of white cloth, fastened by nine buttons of gilt brass on each side. The pattern for these were the same as those worn by captains, a fouled anchor within an oval roped border. No epaulettes were worn by lieutenants at this date. The round cuffs were of white cloth with three buttons the same size as the lapels and collar. The pockets were plain and without decoration and had three buttons. This coat was in fact the same as a captain's but without gold lace, until the new regulations of 1795 altered the captain's uniform entirely. A white single-breasted waistcoat fastened by gilt buttons was regulation for this dress but many young officers adopted short double-breasted waistcoats

23 Lieutenant in full dress uniform with black leather cross belt (*c.* 1805)

which were much more fashionable at this time. White breeches, white stockings and shoes completed the uniform.

The cocked hat was of black felt and without a gold lace binding but did have the gold bullion tassel ornamentation at each end. Swords were carried on a waistbelt underneath the waistcoat, although a painting in the National Maritime Museum, London, depicts a black leather sword belt worn over the right shoulder in the military fashion. The belt plate is an oval shape in gilt metal engraved with a fouled anchor design. A similar plate was manufactured for the Royal Marines and this design is described in *Regimental Badges Worn in the British Army One Hundred Years Ago* by Edward Almack FSA (published in 1900 and republished in a facsimile edition by Frederick Muller Ltd. in 1970). However from a portrait by an unknown artist of a lieutenant in the National Maritime Museum it is assumed it could be the Royal Navy especially as metal was gilded.

Lieutenant 1787–1812. Undress

In undress uniform lieutenants wore a navy-blue cloth coat with a stand-up collar, which was piped around the top in white cloth. In some cases it has been noted from old tailors' books that the collar was sometimes edged at the top and bottom in white and ornamented with a button and button hole on each side.

The coat had blue lapels piped in white on the leading edge and fastened by a row of nine gilt brass buttons of the same pattern used for full dress. Although designed for the lapels to be buttoned back on both sides to display the waist-coat, the junior officers preferred to wear this coat buttoned across leaving the top two or three buttons undone, showing the white cravat. The round cuffs were piped in white and had three gilt buttons on each cuff. The pockets were piped in the same manner showing three gilt buttons also. There were gilt buttons at the waist. Regulations directed that white breeches and stockings would be worn with this dress. However, these junior officers preferred white breeches and black hessian boots except for the most formal occasions. The cocked hat was the same as that worn in full dress.

The sword was suspended from a belt worn under the waistcoat, which was, however, sometimes worn in the more fashionable way of fastening over the coat.

24 A lieutenant (1787–1812) in undress uniform

25 and **26** Midshipman's undress uniform, front and back views (1795–1825)

Midshipman 1795–1825

Midshipmen were placed at an extremely early age by their parents under the patronage of a naval captain, to learn the profession of a Royal Navy officer – in fact the only way to qualify for a commission. Often their names were entered on the ship's books in early childhood. They were the sons of gentlemen, and were to be taught how to be able seamen and manage a ship with skill and to carry out a sea combat with courage and determination.

The uniform for midshipmen changed little from 1787 up to 1825, this consisted of a navy-blue cloth coat cut single breasted with a standing blue collar with a patch of white cloth each side with a brass button set at the back edge. This collar patch was a feature of the 1748 uniform which was the first pattern used by midshipmen and was originally part of the blue collar buttoned back to display the white lining. The coat had nine brass buttons, with fouled anchor but without a roped border. This was in fact the pattern of 1774 used by captains which midshipmen used up to 1812. The blue round cuffs had three buttons, by tradition the reason for three buttons was to prevent them from rubbing their noses on the cuff, when these boys joined the navy they were homesick and longed for the comforts of the shore, most of them had continuous sniffles and were forever rubbing their noses on their cuffs, this was detrimental to the appearance of the uniform, so brass buttons were sewn to the cuff. This also was the basis of the slang expression for midshipmen – 'snotty'.

A white cloth or cassimere waistcoat and breeches was the only regulation dress. But contemporary paintings depict grey breeches for everyday wear. Felt cocked hats were worn athwartships, although at this period round hats or top hats could be seen and are depicted in prints and paintings by Rowlandson, Denis Dighton and Benjamin West. They were sometimes ornamented with a loop of gold lace as shown in Denis Deighton's painting 'The Death of Nelson'. The midshipman's dirk was carried on a black leather cross-belt of the same pattern design as that worn by lieutenants, but this did not last much beyond the Nelson period and the black leather sword belt was more common.

Physician 1805–1825

In May of 1805 the medical branch of the Royal Navy received instructions for a uniform to bring them in line with the army medical service. Since 1787 physicians and surgeons had been dressed as warrant officers. Now, according to a circular sent to medical officers dated 4 June 1805, they were to 'Wear a distinguishing uniform and have a rank similar to officers of the same class in His Majesty's land services, but to be subordinate, however, to that of the lieutenants of the ships and vessels wherein they may be employed.'

The full dress for a physician was to be of navy-blue cloth with a standing collar edged all round in two rows with half inch gold lace. The round cuffs were ornamented with two rows of gold lace of the same width which included three buttons in gilt brass in between the lacing. The design for the button was an anchor but without the cable. Three buttons decorated the plain pockets and the lapels were also plain, fastened by eight buttons in each row. Originally a full dress coat had been suggested with black velvet collar, cuffs and lapels, but this was not adopted. The cocked hats were plain and the waistcoat and breeches were white (with undress uniform blue breeches could be worn). They were, however, not allowed epaulettes, which is the rank of an officer in all navies.

The physicians wrote a letter addressed to the Commissioners of Sick and Wounded Seamen, 'We, the physicians, feel it a duty we owe to the rank we hold in the service and society, to submit to your consideration the claim we have as field officers, to wear epaulettes as have been awarded to officers of similar rank in the staff of the army. We are induced to urge our claim in this respect from being daily liable to meet with army medical officers.' In spite of this appeal the claim was refused and physicians remained without epaulettes during this period.

Surgeon 1805–25

The surgeon's uniform introduced in May 1805 was similar to that of a physician. The coat was of plain navy-blue cloth with a standing blue cloth collar. If the officer was a surgeon of a hospital he was entitled to have two embroidered button holes on the collar, of intertwined gold russia braid. Surgeons serving onboard ships were allowed only one row. There were three gilt buttons on the cuff and eight buttons on each lapel which could be buttoned across if required. The design of the button was a plain anchor within an oval. The letters 'H.S.' were used by hospital staff if they served ashore. The surgeon's full dress uniform (see illustration 27), however, has buttons of the Sick and Hurt office. That is an anchor with a serpent in place of the usual rope design as

27 *(Above)* Full dress uniform of a surgeon (*c.* 1805)

28 *(Above right)* Master (1787–1807), the uniform was worn also by pursers, gunners, boatswain and carpenters

in a fouled anchor. A crown was not added to these buttons until after 1812.

The undress uniform for surgeons was similar to full dress but without buttons on the cuff and a fall-down collar; nor did the coat have pocket buttons. With both uniforms a plain cocked hat was worn of the same pattern and design as physicians.

Dispensers, assistant surgeons and hospital mates were given a single uniform for all occasions of plain blue without lapels with white waistcoats and breeches which could be blue according to choice. Dispensers were allowed the distinction of lapels to their coats.

Warrant Officers 1787–1807

Warrant officers held their appointments or 'warrants' from one of the departments of the Admiralty to supervise certain parts of the ship's company in which they specialized. The master instructed junior officers in the art of navigation as well as being responsible under the captain for the actual sailing of the ship. The purser was appointed with his warrant from the victualling office and was responsible for pay, provisions and the ship's stores. With the gunner, boatswain and carpenter these officers stayed with the ship as long as she lasted, not like the commissioned officers who left with the termination of the ship's commission.

These officers were ordered a uniform in the Dress Regulations of the 17 November 1787, for the first time which remained unaltered until 1807. The coat was of navy-blue cloth with a fall-down collar without ornamentation; the lapels were blue and fastened by brass buttons of design worn by captains previous to their new regulations of 1787 and had the device of a fouled anchor. There were three buttons on the cuff and also on the back pockets. The coat was lined in white but not edged. It had a white cloth waistcoat and breeches. The cocked hat was plain. The appearance was in fact quite civilian as can be seen in the Thomas Rowlandson watercolour of a purser (illustrations 29–31).

The mate's uniform consisted of a blue cloth coat, edged with and without lapels, blue round cuff with three buttons, and three to the pocket. A fall-down collar, the coat lined in white with white waistcoat and breeches. Plain cocked hat.

Ship's company 1805. British sailors

There were no uniform regulations for men of the Royal Navy in 1805, but a style of dress came into favour with the ship's company. That was a straw hat often covered with lacquer or tar, and sometimes with the name of the ship

29 *(Below left)* Ordinary seaman of the period

30 *(Below)* Naval carpenter, with a cauldron of boiling pitch

31 Ship's cook

painted in white letters at the front. A water-colour by the Rev. E. Mangin, Chaplain of the *Gloucester*, depicts a sailor wearing a straw hat with the name 'Gloucester' and a large badge, presumably that of the ship. Pig-tails were worn by the sailors long after they had been discontinued by the officers. The blue jacket had a turned-down collar, and was piped white with usually two rows of brass buttons. The shirt was usually a checkered pattern worn with a cloth round the neck. In action this neckerchief was tied around the head to stop perspiration running into the eyes, and also to cover the ears, the reason for this was that the noise and smoke below decks during action was tremendous, and without protection the sailors' ear-drums would be perforated. The trousers were of linen with a thin blue or red stripe. Although these items could be drawn from the purser's stores little or no attempt was made to encourage uniformity, although in some cases the captains would go to great lengths, and at their expense, to uniform at least some of the ship's company.

The Times newspaper in October 1805 reported 'The *Tribune* frigate, now attached to the Squadron under Sir Sydney Smith, is no less remarkable for its gallantry than the coxcombry of her crew. Every man wears a smart round Japan hat with green inside the leaf, a broad gold lace band, with the name of the ship painted in front in capital letters, black silk neckerchief, with a white flannel waistcoat bound with blue, and over it a blue jacket, with three rows of brass buttons very close together, and blue trousers.'

This amount of uniformity was often confined only to the captain's gig, but also relied on the officer's pocket and his regard for presenting a uniform crew.

The uniform was, however, often decorated personally by the sailors, such as piping in silk the seams of jackets, extra buttons on the coats and of course the painting and decorating of hats.

Water-colours by Thomas Rowlandson show a selection of uniforms worn by British sailors at the time of Trafalgar, which are in fact but little altered from the seventeenth century. For instance the petticoat breeches worn by the ship's cook and the sailor swabbing the deck also date from this time and often incorporated a leather apron to be worn in inclement weather.

The crew were dressed by the slop system, that is certain articles of clothing made to regulations set down by the Royal Navy Commissioners, were sold on board ships by the purser to members of the crew. It was, however, optional for the sailors to buy them.

The Royal Marines 1802–12. Officers

The Marines were made a royal corps by an admiralty order of 29 April 1802, due to the efforts of Admiral Earl St Vincent, a much honoured and loved leader of the Fleet. As was the usual practice with royal regiments the facing colour was altered to royal blue and the lace and metal work to gold or gilt.

It was at Trafalgar that Lieutenant Roteley in the *Victory* was sent to bring up Marines from serving the guns in the middle deck; he wrote 'In the excitement of the action the Marines had thrown off their red jackets and appeared in their check shirts and blue trousers, there was no distinguishing Marine from seamen, all were working like horses.' Helped by the non-commissioned officers he managed to round up twenty-five marines and reached the upper deck to repel boarders just as Captain Adair of the marines was killed and it was also at that time Lord Nelson was fatally wounded and Sergent Major Secker and other marines on Captain Hardy's orders carried the stricken Lord Nelson from the deck of the *Victory*. The marines suffered heavy casualties at Trafalgar, four officers and 113 men killed, with more than 200 wounded. Captain James Atcherley of the Royal Marines was offered the sword of surrender by the French Admiral Villeneuve, commander-in-chief of the French and Spanish fleet on board the French ship *Bucentaure*.

The full dress coat was of scarlet superfine cloth, the standing blue collar decorated with gold-laced button hole and gilt buttons. The lapels were turned back and fastened by gilt buttons. The button holes were sewn with vellum-pattern gold lace. The cuffs were also of blue cloth with three gilt buttons and gold lace decoration. Pockets were ornamented with gold lace and were fitted with three gilt buttons. The turnbacks to the coat were white cassimere. A crimson sash was worn around the waist outside the coat with the tassels hanging on the left side. The gilt buttons had the design of a fouled anchor within a laurel wreath with the words 'Royal Marines' above. White breeches and gaiters were worn for full dress but on other occasions black gaiters were worn. In the Dighton painting of 'The Death of Nelson', white linen trousers are shown to be worn. The cocked hat was bound in black silk and had a gold bullion tassel at each end. On the side a small gilt button held a gold lace ornamentation fastened to a black cockade, from the cockade issued a ten-inch feather plume, red at the base and white at the top.

The sword was supported by a white leather shoulder belt, the plate of which was in gilt brass and engraved with the royal crest; the lion of England standing on the crown. The gorget was engraved with the complete royal coat of arms and motto, with a small shield below containing a fouled anchor, a wreath displayed on each side. Welch and Stalker, the military tailors, described an undress coat made in 1803: 'Superfine scarlet coat cut as regulation. Ten button holes in lapels by twos. Four blue long holes on top of lapels and the rest of the holes on forepart scarlet. Lapel full four inches at top. Blue on each side. Two of a side behind. Four button holes on flaps and cuffs by pairs. White cassimere turnbacks and skirts lined with cassimere. Gold embroidered ornaments heart shape, gold epaulette. Gilt buttons of whatever division they are of – whether Plymouth or Chatham.' Buttons as far as is known are those already described, and divisional buttons appear not to have been used.

Royal Marines 1802–12. Other Ranks

The most characteristic feature of the Royal Marines at this period was the glazed leather hat. The brim was bound in white and was held up on each side by a pair of cords. From a cockade at the left side issued a short plume, red at

32 Royal Marine at the time of Trafalgar (by L.C. Stadlier)

33 Marine Sergeant's coat, back view (*c.* 1805)

34 Sergeant Marine's headgear (*c.* 1805)

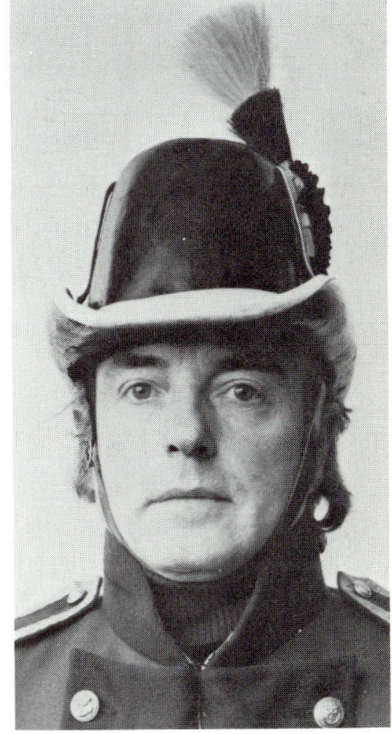

the base and white above. Royal Marine officers did not adopt this headdress until 1812.

The coat was of red cloth, single breasted and fastened by ten buttons set in twos. The button holes were edged in a white tape itself edged in blue and red. The standing collar was of blue cloth and edged in the same tape. On the shoulders the straps were also blue and edged white with a white fringe end. The round cuffs were of blue cloth with four buttons set in twos with an ornamentation of regimental-pattern tape set horizontally. White breeches and gaiters were the order for full dress but on other occasions black gaiters were worn. The Dighton painting depicts the Royal Marines at Trafalgar in white linen trousers but Davidson's painting shows black gaiters. The cross-belts of white leather supported a black leather ammunition pouch on the right hip, the left side held the bayonet. White breeches and gaiters were worn for full dress order, but black gaiters were usually worn on all other duties. Again in the Dighton painting of Trafalgar the marines are shown wearing white linen trousers, two officers are also shown in trousers but these are blue.

Greatcoats, lined with white, were worn also at this time in inclement weather, these were royal blue with a red collar, double-breasted with a cape top. The sword belt was worn over the coat as was the gorget.

British officers' swords at Trafalgar

Vice-Admiral Lord Nelson is presumed to have had two swords in the *Victory* at the time of the battle. Before the action the sword was put out ready for use but apparently he forgot to put it on and it remained in his cabin. It is said one was a dress sword of *c.*1795 and the other a fighting sword of the new 1805 pattern with a shortened blade. During the brief period he was in London before Trafalgar he visited Salter, his sword cutler, and may have bought one of the new-pattern weapons. However, in 1811 Lady Hamilton visited Salter to sell jewellery and plate and is known to have bought a naval officer's sword. This may have been Nelson's new-pattern sword of which he had not taken delivery. Consequently it is not known exactly which sword Lord Nelson had with him at Trafalgar.

A uniform sword for Royal Navy officers was introduced in 1805. An Admiralty minute dated the 4 August states: 'A sword of each pattern to be sent to the Port Admirals at Plymouth, Portsmouth and Sheerness with a

35 Sword of the Master of the Fleet (left) and sword of the mate and midshipman (right)

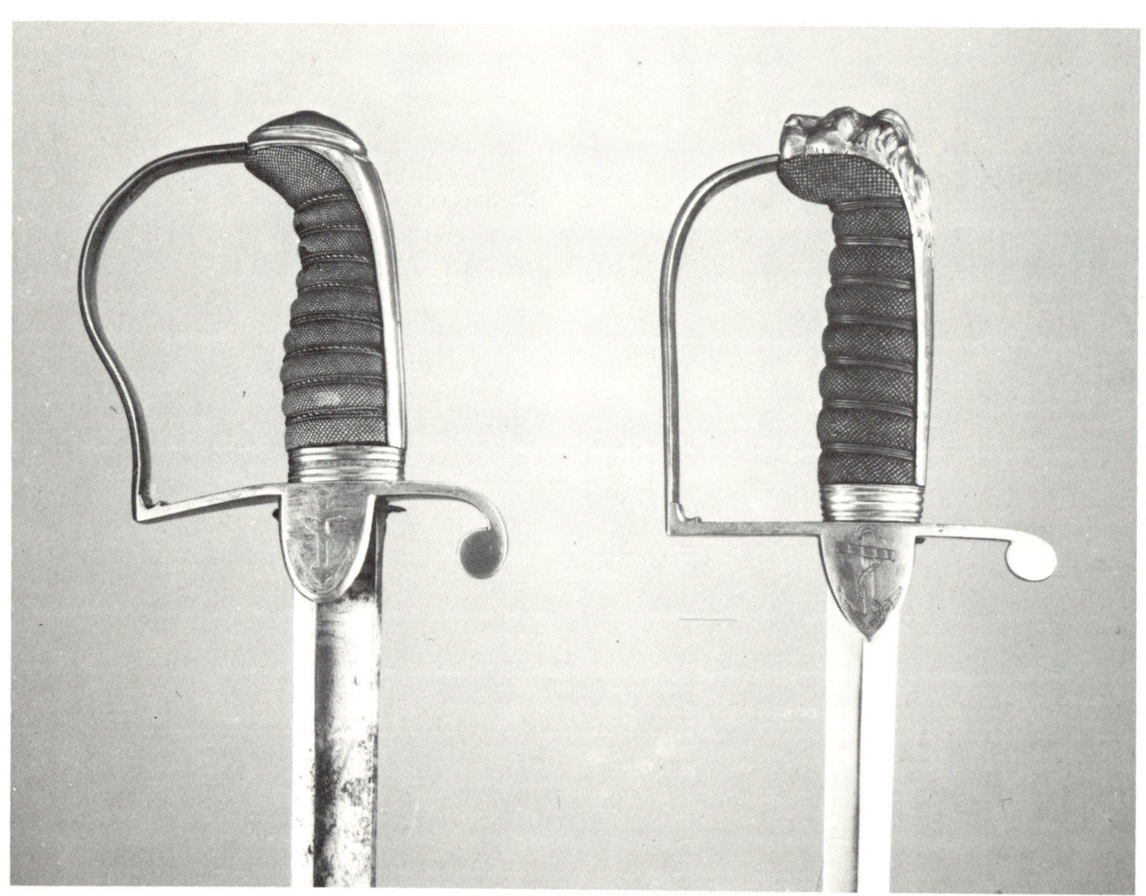

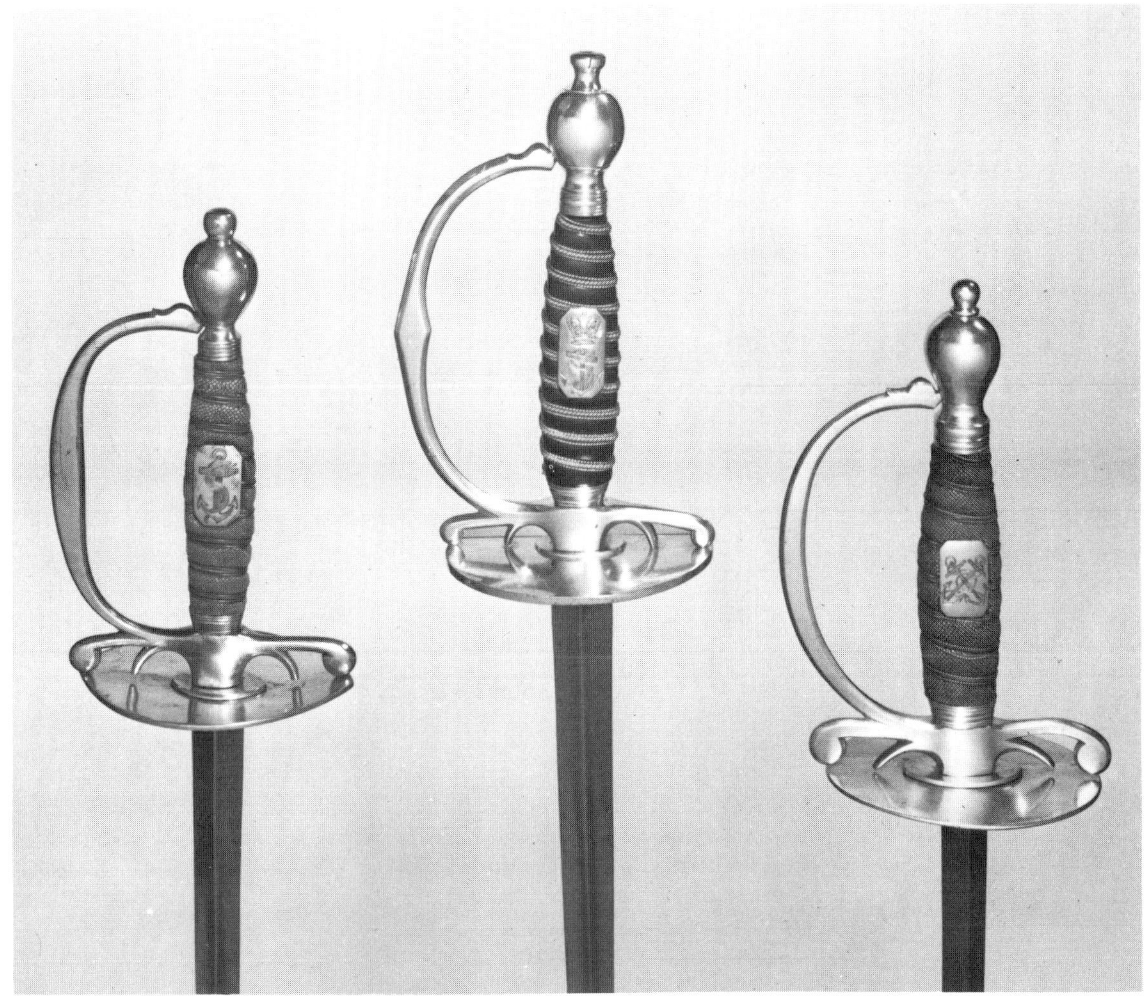

36 Physicians and surgeon's sword (*c.* 1805)

letter signifying the directions of My Lords Commissioners of the Admiralty that they be considered as the uniform swords to be worn in future by officers of His Majesty's Navy.'

The ornamented sword was worn by admirals, captains and commanders and the plain sword by lieutenants and midshipmen. The pommel of the ornamented weapon was in the form of a lion's head, with the mane extending along the back piece. The knuckle guard was plain, in the shape of a stirrup. The langets were engraved with a fouled anchor and the grips were of ivory bound with wire, the whole in gilt metal. Sometimes the grips were in chequered ivory depending on the taste of the owner. The blade, blued and engraved with the royal cypher, masts, flags and anchors, was a straight cut and thrust with a broad groove throughout its length. The scabbard was of black leather with gilt mountings. Lieutenants' swords were the same but with a black sharkskin grip. Midshipmen and warrant officers had a plain pommel and a black sharkskin grip. Deviations to these orders were of course quite common and it is not unusual to find lieutenants' swords with lion's head pommels, and in many cases officers had swords made to their own personal requirements.

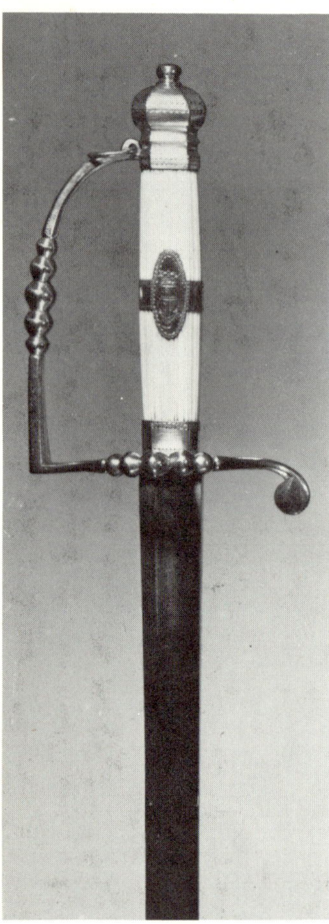

37 Dress sword for flag officers (1790–1805)

Presentation swords of the Patriotic Fund at Lloyds

The Lloyds Patriotic Fund was established on the 20 July 1803 by the underwriters and merchants at Lloyds and took the form of swords of honour. Between 1803 and 1809 when the awards were discontinued, 153 swords had been presented to naval and military officers for gallant and meritorious services. The swords were divided into three classes. Fifty-six were of the value of £100 each; 82 of £50 each, and 15 of £30 each. They were made of silver-gilt with ivory hilts and blades decorated in gold. The swords, complete with a sword belt and sword knot, were presented in a polished mahogany box on which a brass plate was engraved with the owner's name and date of presentation.

The hilt had an ivory grip, diamond knurled and the back piece was a lion's skin in gilt metal. The quillion, a Roman fascia, the knuckle-guard (at right angles to the blade) the club of Hercules with a snake entwined about it and attached to a ring on the lion's mouth. The langets were triangular in the form of a floral pendant, and above them at the base of the grip a plaque with a trophy of arms, cannon, trident and anchor.

The blade was 33-inches long of polished blue damascened steel with designs in gold arranged vertically, the sword-point uppermost. On the obverse side was an inscription relating the reasons for the presentation of the sword and the name of the recipient. Below the inscription was a lion-headed sea monster with fins and a tail supporting a standard, above the inscription was a figure of Victory seated with a wreath and palm branch, rose, thistle, and shamrock flowers; the royal crown and monogram 'GR', within a wreath seated a figure of Britannia; below, Hercules standing with two intertwined dolphins.

On the reverse side of the blade was a rose, thistle and shamrock, a shield engraved with an anchor surrounded by a trophy of arms, Britannia seated, a sea monster, part horse, part dolphin. The royal crown and coat of arms, complete with lion and unicorn supports. Below in a star the recipient's monogram; a phoenix rising from the flames; a figure of Victory within a wreath surmounted by a naval crown; two mermaids each holding a flag inscribed with 'Victory' and the name of the engagement; below, a globe surrounded by a trophy of weapons.

The scabbard was of black leather, mounted in gilt metal. There are three groups of decoration in relief. The designs are the same on both sides and consisted of oval medallions, the first of which (nearest the mouth of the scabbard) shows the British and enemy fleets at Trafalgar in perspective, over which a seated figure of Britannia holds a laurel wreath. The union flag is on Britannia's shield and behind it the mask of a lion. Above the oval on a ribbon was the name of the ship in which the recipient served in the battle surmounted by the stern of a warship flying an ensign, the whole flanked by standards and anchors. Below the oval on a ribbon 'Nelson Trafalgar' and on a circular plate '21st Octr. 1805'. Below this a globe with latitude and longitude indicated. The centre oval design depicts a classical warrior attacking a many-headed monster with a club; around the design are flags, guns, weapons and anchors. The bottom oval design displays Hercules with the Nemean lion, also encircled by flags, guns and anchors. Between the three oval designs are gilt designs in relief exposing the leather scabbard behind. These embellishments consist of a naval crown, helmet, an anchor and buoy, a flag, rudder and floral displays.

The sword belt was of blue leather with floral designs worked all along in gold wire. The belt buckle was an oval clasp in gilt metal, bearing a warrior in classical helmet and carrying an oval shield charged with the union flag. He is killing a dragon with a spear. Below in a scroll 'Patriotic Fund 1803'. Lion head masks are on each side of the buckle and also on the bottom of the belt slings. The rings for the sword belt attachment are in the form of coiled snakes. In the £50 sword the designs in relief between the ovals are omitted and the rings are plain. The sword knot was of blue and gold cord with a gold bullion tassel.

Presentation swords from the Corporation of the City of London

Vice Admiral Lord Collingwood
Captain T. M. Hardy
Rear Admiral the Earl of Northesk
Captain Sir R. Strachan

Presentation swords from the Patriotic Fund at Lloyds

Captain H. W. Bayntun *Leviathan*
Captain Sir E. Berry *Agamemnon*
Captain H. Blackwood *Euryalus*
Captain C. Bullen *Britannia*

Captain E. Codrington *Orion*
Captain J. Conn *Dreadnought*
Captain W. Cumby *Bellerophon*
Captain H. Digby *Africa*
Captain C. Duff *Mars*
Captain T. Dundas *Naiad*
Captain P. C. Durham *Defiance*

Captain R. Grindall *Prince*
Captain E. Harvey *Téméraire*
Captain G. J. Hope *Defence*

Captain R. King *Achille*
Captain Sir F. Laforey *Spartiate*
Captain Lapenotiere *Pickle*
Captain C. M. J. Mansfield *Minotaur*
Captain R. Moorsom *Revenge*
Captain J. N. Morris *Colossus*
Captain I. Pellew *Conqueror*
Captain J. Pilfold *Ajax*
Captain W. Prouse *Sirius*
Captain R. Redmill *Polyphemus*
Captain W. G. Rutherford *Swiftsure*
Captain J. Stockham *Thunderer*
Captain C. Tyler *Tonnant*
Lieutenant R. B. Young *Entreprenante*

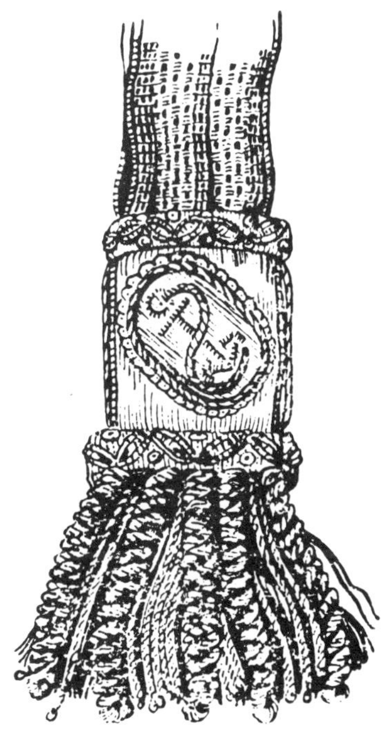

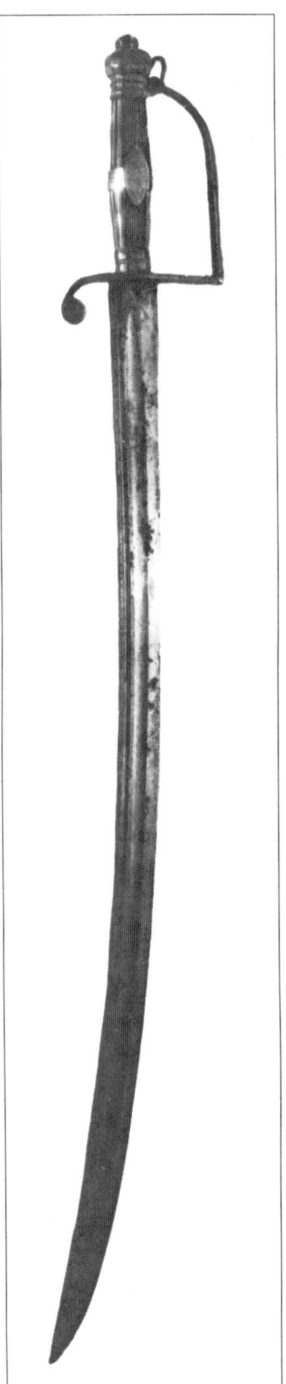

38 Fighting sword of Lord Nelson

39 British Officer's sword knot (*c.* 1805)

The French Navy

Admiral of the Fleet 1805. Full dress

The dress regulations for general officers and admirals of the First Empire were promulgated on the 24 September 1803 and specified the uniforms for general officers, staff officers and other military administrative functionaries. It was ordered that admirals must have a dress and undress uniform.

The full dress coat was of national-blue cloth, lined also in blue. It was single breasted, without lapels and buttoned down to the waist. The tails were cut short. The stand-up collar of scarlet cloth was 70–80mm high, the cuffs were

40 Vice Admiral de Rosily (*c.* 1805)

41 Vice Admiral Allemand (*c.* 1805)

also scarlet, 110mm high, their width exceeding by 10mm that of the sleeve, which was fastened underneath with small buttons. The pockets were set horizontally with three points. On the single-breasted front were nine buttons placed equidistantly from the base of the collar to the level of the pockets. There were three buttons on each pocket, two on the back and two at the end of the tails. The buttons, 27mm across and of gilt brass, were ornamented with a trophy of arms crowned with a helmet and crossed by an anchor. All ranks of admirals had the coat fronts, pockets and tails embroidered 60mm wide. This embroidery represented an oak branch worked in gold wire with spangles on each side of the leaves and piping. The body of the branch and the fine thread of the piping being of gold bullion wire.

The waistcoat has on the front and pockets the same gold wire embroidery as the coatee, but only 35mm wide. It was single breasted and fastened by brass buttons, there were also three buttons on each pocket.

The blue cloth breeches worn with knee boots were without embroidery whilst gala dress had white breeches; stockings with buckled shoes were worn. The garters were embroidered with gold oak leaves.

42 Vice admiral (*c.* 1805)

43 Admiral Bruix in full dress uniform (*c.* 1801)

Admiral of the Fleet 1805. Undress

The undress coat was of national-blue cloth, with collar, cuffs and lining of the same colour with tails overlapping behind and pockets in the folds. The gold-wire embroidery was the same as for full dress, but only 40mm wide. The waistcoat was plain white cloth with gilt brass buttons and the breeches the same as for full dress.

On the undress coat admirals could wear gold epaulettes with twisted fringes. The strap completely embroidered and lined with blue cloth. Silver metal stars which distinguished the rank were placed on the centre portion of the epaulette.

Admirals could also wear a plain coat of national-blue cloth, single breasted, with embroidery only on the collar and cuffs. Epaulettes were worn with this coat. In summer admirals were allowed jacket and trousers of nankeen or striped dimity.

Admirals could also wear a frock coat of national-blue cloth, double breasted, with a stand- and fall-collar, and gauntlet cuffs. The embroidery, only 40mm wide was of one row only and confined to the collar and cuffs. Another optional item was a boat cloak of national-blue cloth with a standing collar embroidered in oak leaves, the border of the cloak also embroidered in the same manner.

The boots for undress uniform were turn-down top boots of yellow leather. When wearing shoes the buckles were of gilt metal.

The sash worn in both full dress and undress was of gold and white netted

44 Vice Admiral C.A. Magon (*c.* 1802)

silk with two tassels with fringed ends on which silver stars were worn denoting the rank of admiral.

The cocked hat for admirals was of black felt bordered by a gold lace 80mm wide. The gold lace braid of the cockade was held by a large gilt button. The ends of the hat were ornamented with twisted gold fringes and decorated with silver stars according to rank. Ranks were also distinguished by silver stars on the epaulettes, on the tassel of the sash and on the sword knot:

Four silver stars for Admiral of the Fleet.

Three silver stars for vice-admiral.

Two silver stars for rear-admiral.

The sash of Admiral of the Fleet was of gold and white silk net. For an admiral gold and scarlet silk and for a rear-admiral gold and sky-blue silk net. Admirals of the Fleet were also accustomed to adding small white plumes to border the cocked hat to indicate their rank.

UNIFORM REGULATIONS FOR THE FRENCH NAVY AT THE TIME OF TRAFALGAR

Uniform of general officers of the marine

Same as the general officers of the army, except that buttons were of gilded metal, representing a 'trophee' crowned with a helmet and crossed by an anchor. 'When the general officers are not onboard ship, they wear the same sword and scabbard as the general officers of the army. When onboard they wear a sabre with an ebony handle, gilded copper ornamentation, and a black scabbard. The belt has the width, design and ornaments as directed for the general officers of the army; but the sabre must not hang lower than 15 centimetres above the ground.'

The belt buckle was gilt and engraved with a relief design of a 'trophee' of arms crossed with an anchor. The sabre belt had two pockets on the inside, to the left and right of the belt buckle to hold two pistols at the waist. General officers wore white collars ashore and black ones on board.

Uniform of marine officers

The captains of ships and frigates had a uniform consisting of full dress and undress.

Full dress: dress coat of national-blue cloth, lined with the same; collar and cuffs of scarlet cloth. Without lapels, buttoned single breasted on the chest to the waist, it hung free over the thighs with a stand-up collar; the cuffs slit and opened behind, the sleeve being fastened with two small buttons; the pockets were fitted crosswise and had three points, the coat flaps falling unfastened behind.

This coat had no edging of piping but was decorated with nine gold button-holes, of silk embroidery in satin-stitch and nine button-holes on each front, two on the collar, three lengthways on each cuff. There were nine large buttons on lapels, three on each pocket, one on each hip, two beneath the pleats, two small ones on each sleeve, and one on each shoulder near the collar to hold the epaulettes. The buttons were of gilded metal, stamped with an anchor.

The waistcoat was of white cloth, the breeches of blue cloth, fastened with small uniform buttons.

Captains wore gold epaulettes with twisted thread fringes; the strap of the epaulettes in plain gold lace and lined with scarlet cloth.

The hat, plain, without plumes, was edged with a strip of goat hair six centimetres wide; the edging of gold lace, 18 millimetres wide, was fixed by a

(*Opposite*) French naval gun crew with a quartermaster. In the foreground is a flexible rammer and sponge, cartridge case, tackle, linstock, a wooden staff with metal fittings to which the slow match is fastened, *c.* 1805. After Edouard Detaille

large uniform button, and there were tassels of twisted thread in the corners of the hat on which there was no piping. The national cockade was worn behind the gold lace decoration.

When ship's captains were not on duty they wore breeches of blue cloth with four small uniform buttons on each side. In summer they were permitted to wear breeches and a jacket of nankeen or white unstriped dimity. Shoe buckles were of silver.

The frock coat was double-breasted of national-blue cloth, as were the collar and cuffs. The pockets were placed longways, in the pleats. Seven heavy buttons on each lapel, one on each hip, two on the pocket straps; the collar was folded down, the cuffs open, being done up by three small buttons, of which two are on the cuff and one on the sleeve. There were two gold buttonholes on the collar.

The cloak was of national-blue cloth, the collar stand-up and edged with gold braid four centimetres wide.

The undress uniform coat was of national-blue cloth, collar, cuffs and

45 Captain of a man-of-war (*c.* 1802)

46 Naval officer's epaulettes (*c.* 1804)

lining of the same; the collar was stand-up, cuffs open underneath being fastened, as was the sleeve, by two small buttons; the pockets were in the tails. This coat was ornamented with buttons as for full dress and had only two gold button-holes on the collar and three longways on each cuff; the waistcoat was of white cloth.

Frigate captains and ship's lieutenants and midshipmen wore the same style and colour of coat as ship's captains.

The full-dress coat of a ship's captain had on each lapel only seven gold button-holes, placed as follows: two at the top, three centrally, and two at the bottom. The distance between the central button-hole and the others was the

(Opposite) Spanish naval captain in the full dress uniform of 1805–1808. On the right is a midshipman with the distinctive gold aiguilette on the right sleeve. Centre is a sailor in working clothes. There was no standard uniform until *c.* 1840

47 Details of gold braid for a naval officer's uniform (*c.* 1804)

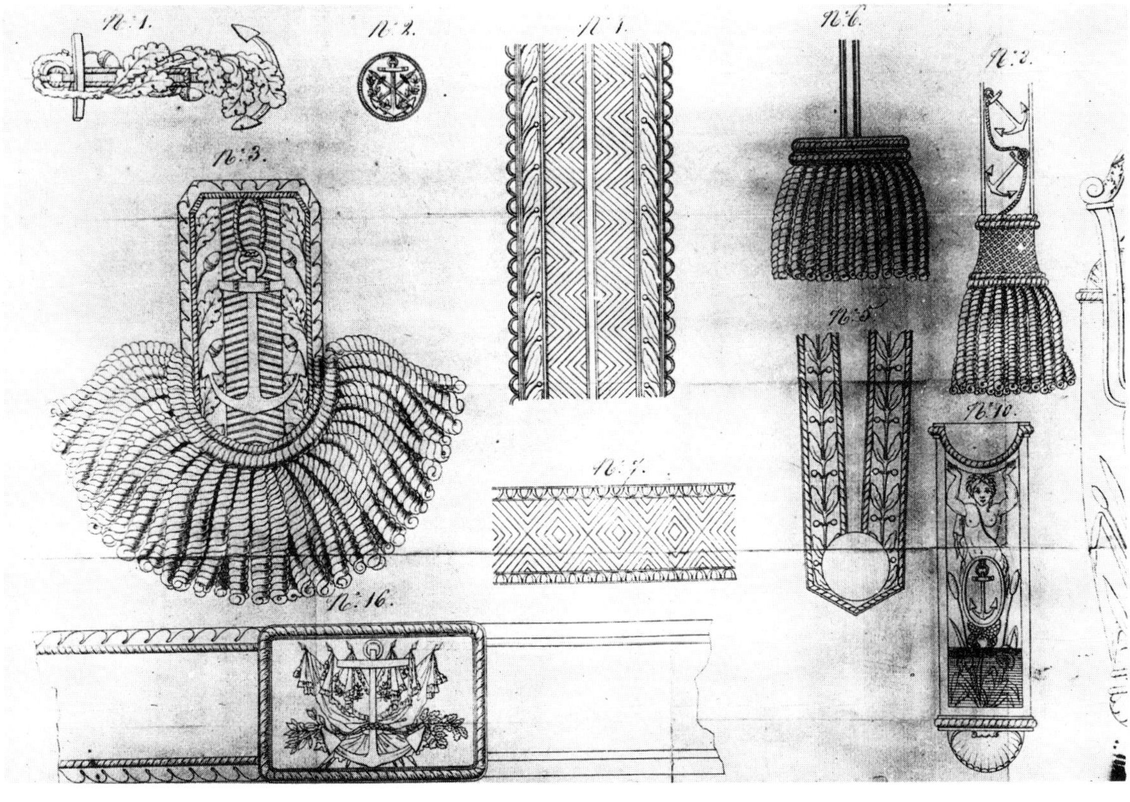

48 Captain Segond, ship-of-the-line (*c.* 1803), undress uniform

same as that of a single button-hole. They also had two button-holes on the collar, three longways on each cuff, and three on each pocket.

Frigate captains wore an epaulette with a twisted-thread fringe on the left shoulder, and an epaulette without a fringe on the right. Their 'undress uniform' was the same as that of ship's captain except for the epaulettes of their rank.

Ship's lieutenants and midshipmen had only two gold button-holes, on each side of the collar of the full dress coat and the undress coat; they were neither put on the lapels nor on the cuffs and pockets. The fringed and unfringed epaulettes, the sword-knot and hat tassels were according to rank.

Armament and equipment

Marine officers of all ranks, when onboard or on duty, wore a sabre with an ebony handle, gilded copper ornamentation and a black scabbard. Ashore they could wear a flat-bladed sword, the handle, guard and ornamentation of gilded metal, and the scabbard black; the sabre and sword were decorated with a gold sword-knot according to rank.

Frigate and ship's captains had a black leather sword belt, six centimetres two millimetres wide, edged with two rows of gold embroidery. Ship's lieutenants and midshipmen had only a single row of gold embroidery. The buckle was of gilded engraved metal.

The sabre belt had two inside pockets to the left and right of the badge to hold two pistols at the waist.

Marine officers, when on board or on duty, were allowed to wear boots. They wore a black collar on board and a white one ashore.

49 Lieutenant of a ship-of-the-line (*c.* 1793)

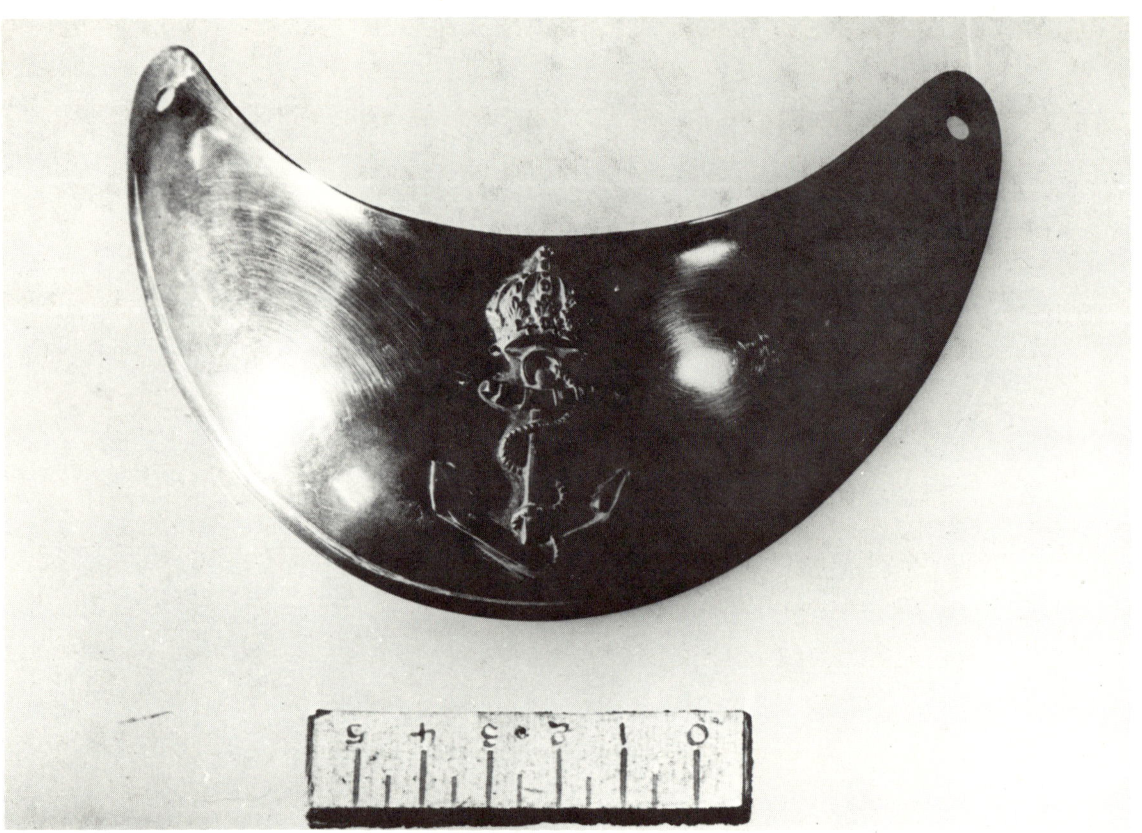

50 Naval officer's gorget (*c.* 1804)

Uniform of staff officers

Military port chiefs, adjutants and sub-adjutants employed there, chiefs of staff, adjutants and deputies embarked with fleets, squadrons and divisions, wore the uniform of their respective ranks in the marine.

Military chief ship's captains, to indicate their duties, wore rear-admiral's plumes on their ship's captain's hats.

Ship's captain's adjutant and frigate captains who acted as military chiefs or adjutants wore a plume without follettes, red, overlaid with white.

Ship's lieutenants adjutant and midshipmen sub-lieutenant, wore a plume without follettes, national blue over-laid with red. 'Follettes' were pliant feathers placed 10–12cm from the top of the plume, taking their name from the way they were ruffled by the wind, and they could be seen above all the plumes of drum-majors, trumpet-majors, officers of light cavalry, hussars and chasseurs.

The general chief of naval forces, if he was not a general officer, would wear a rear-admiral's plume on a ship's captains hat. The adjutant-commandant wore a plume (without 'follettes') – red overlaid with white.

Adjutants and deputies wore on the left arm an armlet – white for adjutants and deputies of admirals or vice-admirals commanding a fleet; sky-blue for those of rear-admirals. These armlets were of cloth with gold fringes, according to rank.

Frigate captains, lieutenants and midshipmen of ships attached to staff, whether ashore or at sea, wore the epaulette of their rank on the right shoulder and the un-fringed epaulette on the left shoulder.

Uniform of the marine administration

The uniform of the marine administration was composed as follows:

Sky-blue coat.

White cloth jacket and trousers.

Buttons of silver-plated metal.

The full dress coat had a sky-blue lining, collar and cuffs of scarlet cloth; it was cut single breasted, fastened by buttons on the chest and hanging free over the thighs; the collar was stand-up, seven to eight centimetres. The cuffs were slit, the pockets fitted cross-wise, the flaps hanging unfastened, and had three points. This coat had nine heavy buttons down the front, three on each cuff, three on each pocket, one on each thigh and two at the bottom of the tails. The front of the waistcoat had small buttons; there are three of these on each pocket and four on each side of the breeches.

51 *(Below left)* Admiral Gourdon in undress uniform (*c.* 1802)

52 *(Below)* Captain of a ship-of-the-line in full dress (*c.* 1804)

Marine administrators were allowed, in 'undress uniform' a coat of the same cloth, of cut and fashion as the full dress coat, with the exception that the pockets were in the tails, the collar turned down, the cuffs open underneath and fastened with two small uniform buttons. Breeches were of sky-blue cloth.

The hat, plain with the national cockade, was edged with a strip of goat's hair six centimetres wide. The left corner of the hat, secured by an edging of silver cord 18mm wide, fixed with a large button behind.

The undress coat was of sky-blue cloth, as were the collar and cuffs; the collar turned down, the pockets in the tails, seven heavy buttons on each front, two on the pocket flaps, one on each thigh; the cuffs were open underneath and fastened with three small uniform buttons.

The cloak was of sky-blue cloth; the collar and edge had an embroidery of the same design as that of the coat but no more than two centimetres five millimetres wide.

53 Captain of a frigate, in full dress (*c.* 1805)

In summer, marine administrators were allowed a jacket and breeches of white unstriped dimity or nankeen; also they could wear boots when in undress uniform.

Marine administrators were distinguished by an embroidered silver design of a vine stock intertwined with an acanthus, around which was a cable; the embroidery in satin-stitch, silver thread, unspangled, three centimetres wide.

The chiefs of marine administration wore, on the full dress coat, two rows of embroidery on the collar, cuffs and pockets. In undress uniform the double rows of embroidery were on the collar and cuffs only. The sword knot was of silver with twisted-thread fringes.

The full dress coat of principal commissioners had a double row of embroidery on the collar, cuffs and pockets; but the first row of embroidery was only half as wide as the second.

The undress coat was the same as that of the chiefs of marine administration, except that the first row of embroidery was only half as wide as the second.

The undress coat of marine commissioners was edged with a single row on the collar and cuffs and pockets; the undress coat and the frock coat had only one row of embroidery on the collar and cuffs; the sword knot silver, with twisted thread fringes.

The full-dress coat of deputy commissioners of the marine was embroidered on the collar and cuffs only; on the undress coat and frock coat there was only one row of embroidery on the collar and cuffs; the sword knot silver with twisted-thread fringes.

The full dress coat of deputy commissioners of the marine was embroidered on the collar only a silver twist and a silver button-hole whilst the silver sword knot, with thread fringes had in the middle of the cord a strip of sky-blue silk one centimetre wide.

Marine stewards wore a plain sky-blue cloth coat, with the marine administration button.

The weapon used was the French sword; the handle, guard and ornament of silver-plated metal with a black scabbard. The sword-belt, six centimetres two millimetres wide was of black leather, edged with silver embroidery; the belt buckle silver-plated copper with an engraved design. In full dress the sword-belt was worn over the jacket.

Uniform of marine inspectors

The uniform of marine inspectors was composed as follows:

The coat of national-blue cloth, lined with red serge.

Waistcoat and breeches of white cloth.

Blue collar.

Cuffs of scarlet cloth.

The buttons of silver-plated metal.

The full dress coat buttoned single-breasted on the chest and hung free over the thighs. The collar of the same cloth, stand-up; the cuffs, of scarlet cloth, were fastened with hooks and eyes. The pocket flaps were three-pointed, fitted crosswise, hanging unfastened. This coat was single-breasted, ornamented with nine heavy buttons, three on the cuffs, three on each pocket, one on each hip, and two at the bottom of the tails. The waistcoat and breeches were ornamented with small uniform buttons.

The plain hat was edged with a strip of black goat's hair; six centimetres wide. The silver 'galon' was 18mm wide and fixed by a heavy button, behind which was the national cockade. Silver shoe buckles were worn.

54 *(Above)* Naval officer in his cloak (*c.* 1805)

55 *(Above right)* Lieutenant of a ship-of-the-line, in his great-coat (*c.* 1804)

The undress coat was cut, styled, and lined in the same way as the full-dress coat, except that the pockets were in the tails, the collar was turned down and the cuffs opened underneath, fastened with two small uniform buttons. The breeches were of the same cloth as the coat.

Frock-coats were of the same cloth as the coat, as were the collar and cuffs; the collar turned down; the cuffs and sleeves open behind and were fastened with three small uniform buttons; the pockets in the tails. The frock-coat was double breasted and fastened with seven heavy buttons placed equidistant, there were buttons also on each thigh and two on the pocket flaps. In summer the inspectors were allowed jacket and breeches of white dimity or nankeen.

The cloak was of national-blue cloth. The stand-up collar and edge had the same embroidery as the coat but not wider than two centimetres five millimetres. Marine inspectors were allowed boots when on duty.

On the full-dress coat marine inspectors had an embroidery of an oak branch intertwined with palm leaves, all encircled with a cable and wore a sash when on duty.

The embroidery of the coat was satin-stitch in silver thread, unspangled; three centimetres two millimetres wide, including the embroidered edging. The coat was embroidered on the collar pockets and cuffs but had no embroidery on the fronts or on the tails. In undress uniform and on the frock coat there was a band of embroidery on the collar and cuffs.

The sash of plain sky-blue taffeta silk had at each end three centimetres of embroidery satin-stitch in silver thread, unspangled; and decorated with an eight-centimetre fringe of thread and twisted thread, silver; the sword knot was of silver with twisted thread fringes.

Marine deputy inspectors had only one row of embroidery on the collar and cuffs; in undress uniform and on the frock-coat there was only one row of embroidery – on the collar. The sash was green; the sword knot silver. Swords were of marine officer's pattern, the handle, guard and ornament silver plated metal; the scabbard was black. The sword belt was of black leather, six centimetres two millimetres wide, and edged with two plain rows of embroidery, worked in silver satin-stitch; the belt buckle, engraved silver-plated metal.

Uniform of half-pay general officers, marine officers, administrators, and marine inspectors

Half-pay generals wore a national-blue cloth coat, lined with the same, blue collar and cuffs, white waistcoat and blue breeches. This coat was single breasted and had a stand-up collar, cuffs slit and open underneath, the sleeve fastening by two small buttons, pockets crosswise and three-pointed, and decorated, as was the jacket and breeches, with uniform buttons of the style of general officers of the marine.

Half-pay generals had no embroidery, nor did they wear a sash, they were recognized by silver-wire stars embroidered on their epaulettes, and a gold sword knot, according to their respective rank.

The hat was edged with gold lace of a general officer and worn without plumes; the national cockade the only decoration. Swords were those of a general officer of the army.

Half-pay ship and frigate captains, ship's lieutenants and midshipmen, wore a uniform coat of national-blue cloth, lined with the same, collar and cuffs of crimson velvet; waistcoat of white cloth and blue breeches. These were all decorated with uniform buttons; they also wore the epaulettes and sword-knot of their rank. They had no gold button-holes on this coat or on the frock-coat.

Half-pay marine chiefs of administration, principal commissioners, commissioners and deputy commissioners, wore plain, unembroidered coats of sky-blue cloth, collar and cuffs of crimson velvet. Waistcoat and breeches of white cloth; uniform marine administration buttons and the sword knot of their rank.

Marine inspectors and deputy inspectors wore, in uniform, a coat of national-blue cloth, single-breasted, and lined with red serge, with a collar of white cloth and uniform buttons of marine inspectors. There was no embroidery on this coat and the sword-knot was according to their respective rank.

If they were receiving no pay, or had given in their resignation, the above ranks were not allowed to wear any uniform whereas officers of all ranks on retirement pay could wear a uniform composed of a coat of national-blue cloth, lined with scarlet serge, white waistcoat, blue breeches. This coat was single-breasted; the collar and cuffs of blue cloth; the collar stand-up, the cuffs fastened with hooks and eyes, the pockets crosswise and three-pointed. The coat was decorated with three buttons on the cuffs, nine down the front, one on each hip, and two at the bottom of the tails. The coat tails could not be turned up behind. The waistcoat and breeches were decorated with small uniform buttons.

A plain black hat ornamented with the national cockade and a gold braid fixed by a button, edged with a strip of goat's hair six centimetres wide was worn.

The uniform button of gilded metal, stamped with two wreaths, of oak and laurel, intertwined and crossed by an anchor was the regulation. The sword, epaulettes and sword-knot were of their respective ranks.

Senior medical officers

For all medical officers the coat was of bright blue cloth with a lining of the same material; the collar and cuffs were of black velvet for doctors, scarlet for surgeons and dark green for apothecaries. This coat, single-breasted, hung free over the thighs and crossed behind. The collar, stand-up, eight centimetres high, the cuffs fastened with hooks and eyes, the pockets crosswise were three-pointed. The coat was fastened with nine heavy uniform buttons, three on the cuffs, three on the pockets, one on each hip and two at the bottom of the tails.

The uniform button of medical officers was of gilded metal, stamped with an anchor around which was the serpent of Epidaurus, and surrounded by a branch of oak and laurel.

The waistcoat for doctors was of the same material as the coat; for surgeons

56 Naval officers of *c.* 1798

of scarlet cloth; for apothecaries of dark-green cloth; and decorated with uniform buttons.

Breeches for all medical officers were of the same cloth as the coat, and decorated with four small buttons on each side. In summer, medical officers were allowed to wear jacket and trousers of white dimity or nankeen.

The hat was plain, edged with a strip of goat's hair six centimetres wide. The braid of gold 'lace' 18mm wide fixed by a heavy uniform button and the national cockade but without other ornament.

Medical officers could wear, in undress uniform, a coat of the same cloth, having the collar and cuffs of velvet of the colour of their respective profession; all cut and finished in the same way as the full-dress uniform coat, but with the following exceptions: the collar was turned down, the sleeve opened underneath and fastened by two small uniform buttons; the pockets were in the tails and could not be seen.

The frock coat was of the same cloth as the coat, double breasted and decorated with seven heavy uniform buttons on each row, one on each hip, and two on the pocket flaps which were longways in the tails. The cuffs fastened by three small buttons. The collar and cuffs were of velvet, the colour indicating the respective professions.

The cloak, of the same cloth as the coat had an edging of gold lace four centimetres wide. The collar velvet, the colour indicating the professions. Boots had turned down tops of yellow leather whilst shoes had silver buckles.

The sword was of gilded metal, uniform with that of infantry of the line and the sword belt of black patent leather six centimetres wide. The belt buckle was gilded.

Medical officers were distinguished according to their professions and

57 Admiral Magendie in undress uniform (*c.* 1805)

classes by gold embroidery around the button-holes representing acanthus leaves round which was the serpent of Epidaurus, and by the sword-knot. These had silk stripes on the cord of the sword-knot to distinguish the rank of medical officers, black for doctors, red for surgeons, green for apothecaries.

Chief doctors, surgeons and apothecaries

This coat was edged on the fronts, collar, cuffs and pockets with gold braid, three centimetres two millimetres wide. The waistcoat was similarly edged with braid two centimetres wide and on the undress uniform coat and the frock coat there was a single row of lace on the cuffs and collar. There was a gold sword-knot with twisted thread fringes.

Assistant doctors, surgeons and apothecaries

The coat was decorated with lace the same as senior medical officers, but not put on the collar, cuffs and pockets. The waistcoat was edged with lace and on the undress uniform coat and the frock coat a single row of lace on the collar only, was the only decoration. A gold sword-knot with twisted-thread fringes was worn.

Instructors

Nine gold braid button-holes, two centimetres wide, on each front of the coat, two on the collar, three longways on the cuffs, three on the pockets. The jacket edged with gold lace two centimetres wide.

On the undress uniform coat and the frock coat, there were two button-holes on the collar and three on each cuff. The waistcoat was edged in lace. The gold sword-knot, with twisted-thread fringes, had in the centre of the braid a strip of silk six millimetres wide.

Medical officers

First class medical officers had nine gold braid button-holes on each coat front, two on the collar, three on the cuffs and three on the pocket flaps.

On the undress uniform coat and the frock-coat there were two on the collar and three on the cuffs. There was a gold sword-knot with thread fringes.

Those of the second class had two button-holes on the collar, three on the cuffs, three on the pocket flaps, but not put on the coat fronts. On the undress uniform coat and the frock coat there were two button-holes on the collar only. Gold sword-knot, a six millimetre wide strip of silk down the centre of the cord, thread fringes.

Those of the third class had two button-holes on the collar, three on the cuffs; they were not put on the pockets. On the undress uniform coat and the frock coat, a single button-hole on the collar but none on the cuffs. There was a gold sword-knot with thread fringes, the cord having on the two sides a four millimetre wide strip of silk.

Auxilliary medical officers and midshipmen wore a coat, waistcoat, breeches, collar and cuffs prescribed above; all decorated with uniform buttons, but without gold button-holes or braid. The edge of the cloak was not laced.

Half-pay medical officers were allowed to wear the uniform prescribed above, except that the collar and cuffs were in all cases of crimson velvet, and on the coat, jacket and frock coat no lace or gold button-holes.

If receiving no pay, medical officers could not wear uniform.

Ship's company 1805

The French naval uniforms for crew were appointed by military decree in 1804. The dress consisted of a black glazed hat decorated at the side with a rosette of the national colours, held by a strap of gold lace and a brass button. On the front was a gold-painted anchor. The short jacket was of blue cloth with a turned-down collar and lapels, the front ornamented with two rows of brass buttons, the cuffs had three buttons but no other ornamentation. The trousers were also of blue cloth and the waistcoat was red, single-breasted and fastened by a row of six brass buttons. Shoes and socks were worn in port and on land.

Boatswains were ordered a black cocked hat and a blue tail coat which had stand-up collars in the colour of their appointments. The quartermaster's chevrons were also in coloured cloths to denote to which department they belonged:

navy blue – working the ship, that is the actual sailing of the vessel
red – ship's gunners
gold – pilots
crimson – carpenters and caulking
white – sail-makers
black – armourers and blacksmiths
light blue – pursers

58 Quarter-master (*c.* 1805)

59 *(Above)* Ordinary seaman (*c.* 1793)

60 *(Above right)* Lieutenant of a man-of-war (*c.* 1793)

Ranks denoted by chevrons were: sergeant majors, sergeants, second mates, corporals and quarter-masters.

Petty officers wore a sword at all times when in uniform, but the ordinary crew members were only armed at their combat stations with cutlass, and when necessary the boarding pike and axes. These weapons were kept on the main-deck of the ships around the masts, held in stands.

61 Marines of 1800–05

62 Sailor's hat (*c.* 1805)

63 Naval non-commissioned officers, helmsman, quarter-master carpenter, quarter-master sails

64 *(Above left)* Marine Officer of the Guard (*c.* 1805)

65 *(Above)* Marine of the Guard (*c.* 1805)

French marine artillery troops

The equipment issued to each soldier on his arrival at the corps was:

In the knapsack:

Three shirts
Three handkerchiefs
One pair of black gaiters
One pair of grey linen gaiters
Two pairs of shoes
Three pairs of stockings
Two collars
Powder pouch, brushes, combs, buckles, pigtail ribbons, and priming iron.

66 Gunner and drummer of the Marines (*c.* 1796)

Military worker of the marine

The order of 27 April 1800 organized the marine service. The shore of France was divided into six prefectural regions, and port and arsenal duty became regulated in a precise manner.

A consular order of the 26 September in the same year established, for the instruction of young seamen, four companies of apprentice gunners: two at Brest, one at Rochefort, and the last at Toulon.

On 1 July 1802 the marine corps included, besides seven half brigades of artillery, three companies of workers. Twenty companies of conscript marine workers were created on the 14 March 1803 and for service in this army a levy of 2000 conscripts was ordered. On the 5 June 1805 the 20 battalions forming the seven half brigades of marine artillery were reduced to 12, which took, on the 9 December 1805, the denomination of Imperial Corps of Marine Artillery.

One hundred companies (which soon increased to 145 of cruiser gunners) were created by the order of 28 May 1803, each composed of 120 men and two officers. They were entrusted especially with the defence of the coasts and the offshore islands. The companies of conscript workers were reduced to 18 on the 15 January 1808, and took the name Military Workers of the Marine.

Two consular orders dated from the 13 December 1811 and the 19 February 1812 ordered 40,000 seamen to be used in the Russian campaign.

67 *(Below left)* Marine of the Guard (*c.* 1803)

68 *(Below)* Marine of the Guard (*c.* 1804)

French officers' swords at Trafalgar

Several different pattern swords were used in the battle of Trafalgar. One pattern was introduced in 1800 and a variant was adopted on 15 June 1805. Coupled with the fact that officers were using swords previous to these regulations, it is difficult to date swords other than those which have a definite history or were captured and surrendered at Trafalgar.

Flag officers wore a sword very similar to those of army generals, with a stirrup-hilt all gilt, the head of Medusa on the langet and the head of a lion on the back piece. Army generals had a steel scabbard, but for naval service this was replaced by one of leather with gilt-brass mountings.

For dress occasions an epée was used by flag officers. This had a shell guard in gilt metal, heart shaped, edged in laurel leaves and with the face of a roman soldier and in the centre of the cross-piece there was a shield decorated with a sun-burst. On the knuckle guard was a star to denote the rank of admiral. The scabbard was of black leather with gilt mountings.

The sword of Captain J. J. Magendie of the *Bucentaure*, now in the collection of the National Maritime Museum, London is of the 1800 pattern with a straight stirrup hilt in gilt metal, a fluted pommel and a knurled ebony grip. The end of the quillions are decorated with a lion's head, the large langets have a cast design of a fouled anchor. Magendie's sword was captured by a Captain Thomas Fremantle, later Vice-Admiral Sir Thomas Fremantle GCB, who commanded the *Neptune* at Trafalgar. Another sword of this type is to be seen at the National Maritime Museum, London, and is exactly the same as the army pattern, the only difference being the fouled anchors on the langets.

The sword of Captain L. A. Baudoin who was killed at Trafalgar in the *Fougueux* has an all-brass stirrup hilt, with a black horn grip bound with wire.

70 *(Below right)* Naval sword from the *Bucentaure* (*c.* 1805)

69 (*Below*) Naval sword from the *Fougueux* (*c.* 1805)

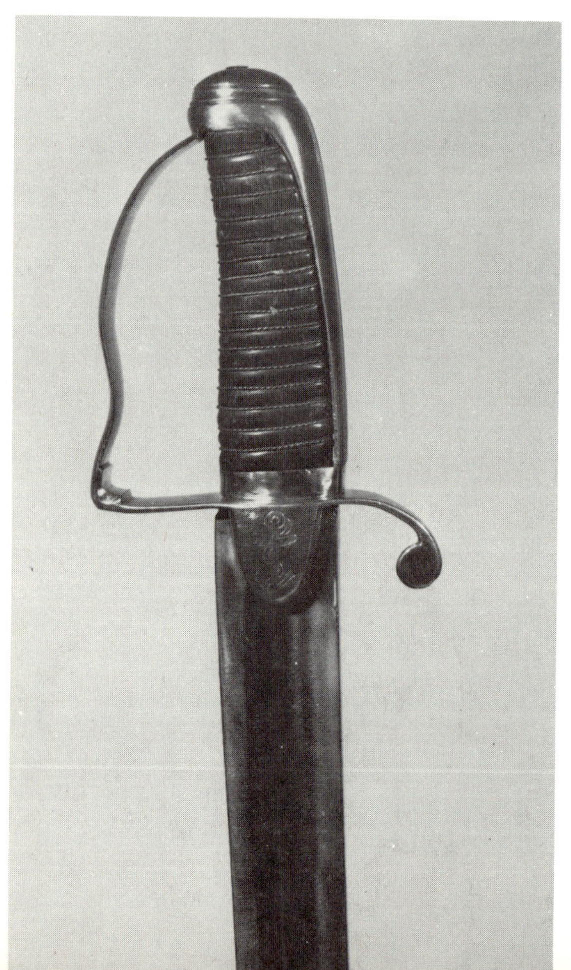

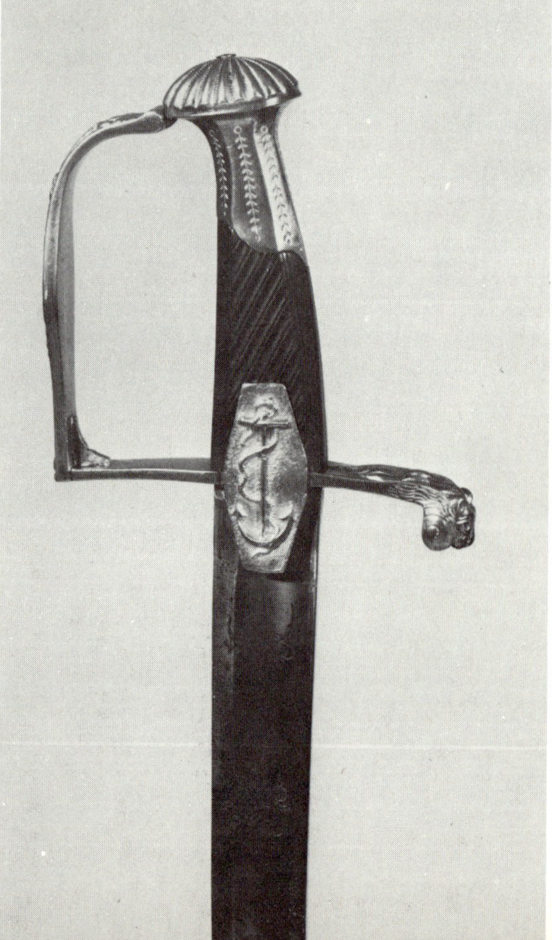

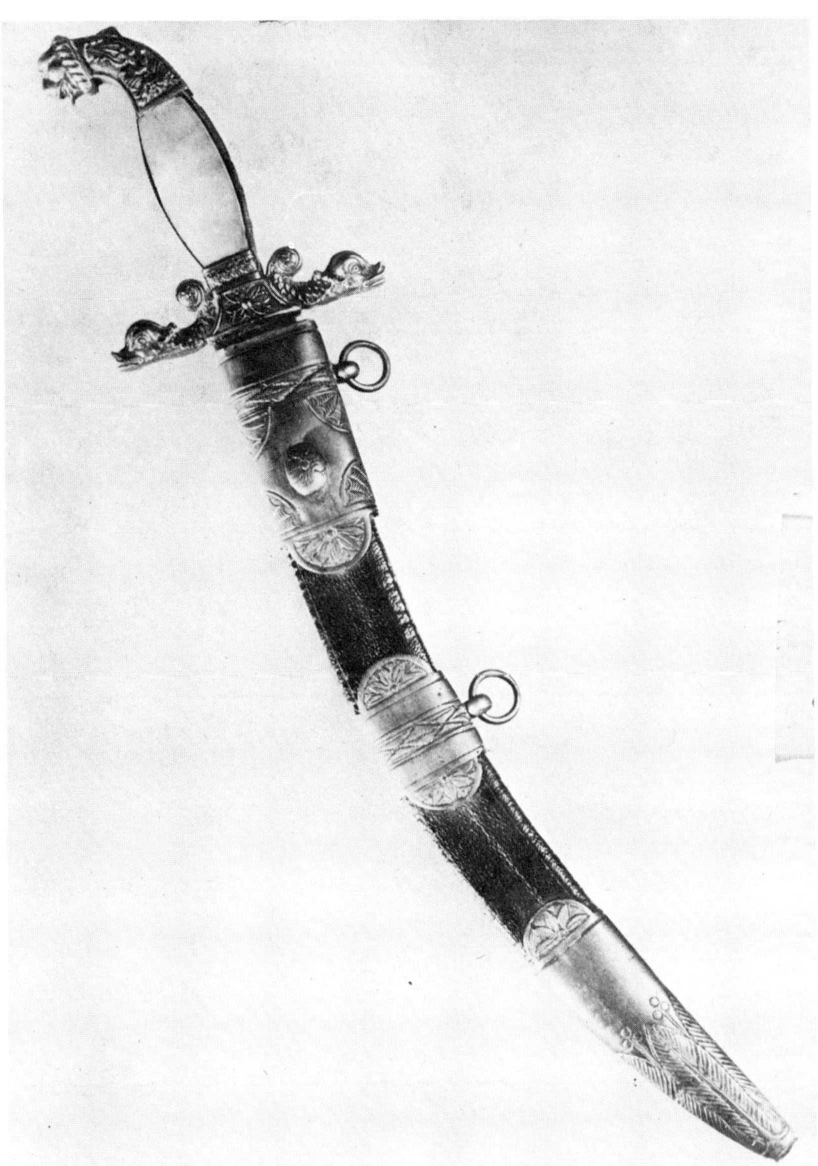

71 Naval dirk (Egyptian Campaign)

The langets are engraved with a fouled anchor and cable. The blade is falchion shape and very curved. Captain Infernet of *L'Intrépide* was obliged to yield when seven British ships had engaged him, killing half the crew and dismasting the ship. His sword, also at the National Maritime Museum is of the army pattern, the langets are engraved 'L'Intrépide', '74' and 'Trafalgar October 21st 1805'.

The sword of Admiral Villeneuve, commander in chief of the combined fleets of France and Spain was surrendered to Vice-Admiral Lord Collingwood. This sword is now in the Nelson collection at Monmouth. It is of a pattern carried by French generals and has a knight's helmet as a pommel and a flattened grip board in silver wire. The knuckle-guard is decorated with laurel leaves with a star at the centre. It has straight quillons with lions' heads at the

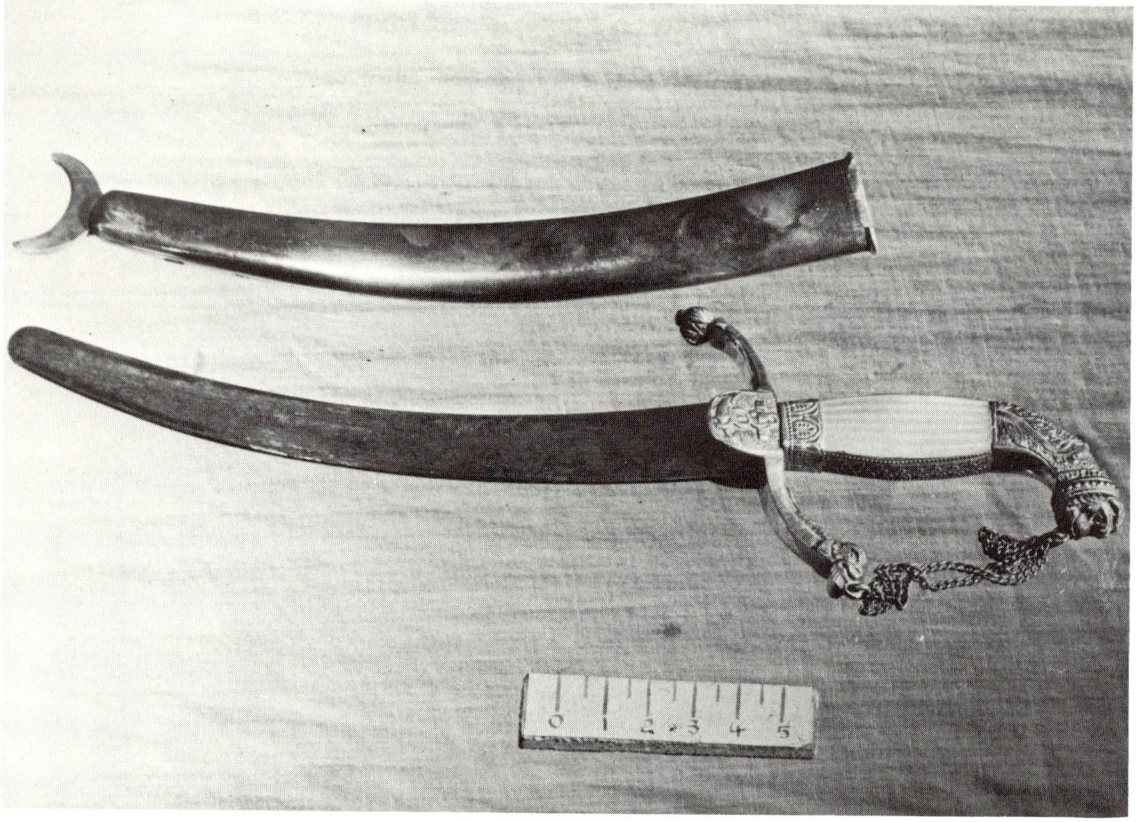

72 Naval dirk (Egyptian Campaign)

73 Naval speaking trumpet in copper with a silver mouth piece (*c.* 1798)

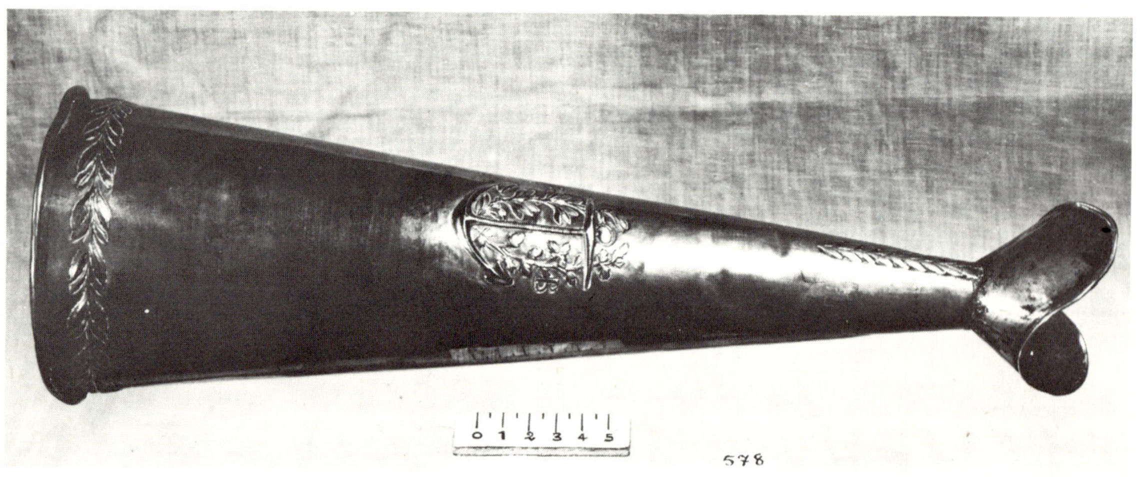

ends and the flat shell-guard is surrounded by laurel-leaf decoration. The diamoned-sectioned blade is $32\frac{1}{2}$-inches long. The unusual feature is the absence of anchors or any other naval motif. The admiral surrendered his sword to Lieutenant Hennah, the senior surviving officer in the *Mars*.

Civil branches of the French navy wore an epée sword, usually with a silver hilt, the knuckle-guard decorated with a dolphin and the pommel urn shaped. Medical officers wore the army pattern sword. The epée varied considerably in design, a fine example of *c.* 1805 has an ivory hilt with a roman helmeted warrior as the pommel, the knuckle-guard is decorated with laurel leaves. A lion's head in the centre. On the shell-guard there is a trophy of flags, with the figure of Victory leaning on an anchor. The exact rank or branch of the French navy is unknown.

Franch navy cutlasses at Trafalgar

In the year XI (1802–03) a new cutlass was introduced for service with the French navy. The blade was $1\frac{1}{2}$-inches wide with a broad fuller and was $29\frac{7}{8}$-inches long. The octagonal grip was covered with sheet iron on a wood base. An oval shell made of iron contacted to form the knuckle-bow which fitted to the pommel of an octagonal shape. The half basket guard was of iron and painted black and covered the hand. The trailing end of the shell terminated in a leaf shape with five laps, because of the shape of this cutlass, it was called the cuillere á pot by the French sailors.

French naval dirks

The use of this weapon was not authorized in the French navy, although the dirk was often worn by officers in place of a sword on certain occasions. At Trafalgar some such dirks were captured, one has the part blade of a Genoese small sword and has a five-ball side-ring and the usual type of straight hilt. This was taken in *L'Intrépide* at Trafalgar. Another has a straight blade with a cross-hilt with an embossed anchor in the centre and an ivory grip. The weapon is engraved 'Vaincre ou mourir pour la nation la patrie'. A third dirk at the National Maritime Museum was once the property of Vice-Admiral Lord Collingwood. The grip is of square knarled ebony, all the fittings are silver gilt, the pommel semi-spherical with spiral flutings. The cross-piece has an oblong block with acorn ends, the chain knuckle guard is missing. The scabbard is of black leather with silver-gilt mounts and was made by Pierre Nicolas Somme at Paris in about 1798.

The Spanish Navy

Flag officer's full dress

The coat was of navy-blue cloth with a standing collar of red. This collar was edged all round in an escalloped design of gold-wire embroidery. The body of the collar was completely covered in gold embroidery, the design of which was continued through the lapels and cuffs. This consisted for admirals of three bands of gold encircled by a continuous single row of oak leaves. The coat was worn buttoned across the chest with the top buttons undone to display the lapels on each side of the chest, showing the red lining. The edge of the lapels were embroidered in gold wire in the same pattern as the collar but were, in addition, embroidered on the right front side, so that the embroidery was visible from both sides even when the coat was fastened across the chest. The deep-red cuffs had an escalloped gold edge at the top, and for admirals three bands of embroidery encircling the cuff. Around the waist was worn a scarlet sash fastened on the left hand side with two heavy bullion gold tassels and above the fringes were three rows of embroidery in the oak leaf pattern. The waistcoat was not visible unless the coat was worn with both lapels buttoned back in the more old-fashioned manner. The waistcoat was of red cloth fastened by a single row of brass buttons. The breeches in full dress were white with white stockings and shoes.

The cocked hat was edged all round in a broad gold lace and the red silk cockade, the national colours at the time, was fastened by a twist of gold thread; from behind the cockade issued a red feather plume. Special mention should be made of the cross on the chest, embroidered in red silk and worn over the heart. They were stuffed with tightly folded miniature prints of saints and prayers. This uniform, although altered to follow the dictates of civilian fashions remained ostensibly the same throughout the eighteenth century and into the nineteenth.

The sword belt worn under the sash was of gold lace lined with red morocco leather and fitted with gilt fasteners.

Flag officer's undress. 1805

This coat was of blue cloth with a standing collar of the same material. It was edged, as were the lapels, with a plain gold russia braid. The lapels were of red cloth and could be worn open or closed. Generally the coat was worn with the top buttons undone to display the red lapels as in the full dress garment. The lapels were embroidered in gold as on the full dress coat, but the collar was plain. The cuffs were the same as for full dress. With this uniform was worn the red waistcoat with a single row of brass buttons, red knee breeches, white stockings with black buckled shoes. The cocked hat was the same as that worn

74 Flag officers of *c.* 1805

with the full dress, although the red plume was usually removed. This was the uniform worn by admirals for day-to-day wear and onboard during an action at sea.

Captain's full dress. 1805

The coat was of navy-blue cloth, cut with tails slashed to the waist at the back and with coat falling away at the hips in front. The collar was of red cloth and is shown in some paintings of the period as being of the stand-and-fall type. This was, however, an earlier fashion and the paintings probably illustrate old uniforms being worn out which was quite common in all countries. The facing of the collar is red and edged all round in gold lace. The lapels which can be buttoned back, are red, bound on the outer edge with a gold lace. The buttons were gilt brass.

In full dress the lapels were buttoned back all the way to the waist to display the red linings. The pockets were three pointed and edged all round including the top with gold lace. Three gilt buttons were placed under the flap. Two further buttons were placed in the waist line at the back of the coat. The tails were square ended and were not fastened back. The cuffs were of red cloth with circular rings of gold lace to denote rank. The waistcoat was of the same pattern as for flag officers and made of red cloth single breasted and fastened by a row of gilt brass buttons. The breeches were also red cloth secured at the knees by four small gilt buttons. White stockings and black buckled shoes were worn in this order of dress. In some cases officers wore black calf-length

75 Admiral Don Federigo Gravina (*c.* 1805)

76 Left to right: naval infantry in undress (aboard ship); naval artillery in undress (aboard ship); naval infantry in full dress (on shore) and naval artillery in full dress (on shore)

boots, lined in red and with a red top edge. These however, were unofficial. The black felt cocked hat edged all round with a broad gold lace, and at the crest of the hat was worn the red cockade of Spain, and a red plume. The sword was suspended from a waistbelt worn under the waistcoat.

Captain's undress. 1805

This blue cloth coat was cut with tails. The collar was plain blue also. The coat was double breasted and lined in red. The buttons were gilt brass and it was the fashion to leave the top buttons undone with the lapels turned back to display the red lining.

The round cuffs were red with the top edge bound with a single row of gold lace. The red breeches were worn with white stockings and buckled shoes. Junior officers sometimes affected black top boots, following the general fashion in other navies of Europe. The cocked hat that was worn for full dress was also used with this uniform, sometimes without the plume.

Midshipmen 1805

The bicorne hat of a midshipman was of black felt, bound with a gold lace, from the red silk cockade issued a red feather plume. The coatee was of blue cloth with a standing collar. The coatee was single breasted with two rows of seven brass buttons, which allowed the lapels to be buttoned back. It was, however, the custom by this date to button back only the top of the lapels. The collar and the turnbacks were red. The coatee also had plain red cuffs. The lapels were edged all round in a gold lace, on the right shoulder was worn a gold plaited aguillette with gilt brass ends, this was the distinctive rank of a midshipman. The waistcoat was red lined, double breasted with brass buttons. The sword belt was worn under the belt and had a brass buckle ornamented with a crown and anchor design. The belt was of black morocco leather. The breeches were blue cloth or white for full dress occasions. With black boots. Hungarian style. Off duty midshipmen were allowed blue trousers and shoes or white breeches, stockings and black buckled shoes.

Naval artillery 1805

The uniform for the Spanish naval artillery was very similar to that of the Naval Infantry with only a few differences. The bicorne hat was of black felt, bound in black edging. The plume was of red feathers and the cockade was of red silk, the Spanish national colour.

The coatee was of blue cloth, single breasted with a plastron front. The standing collar was red. The turn-back lapels were blue and piped in red, these were fastened by a row of six brass buttons. The cuffs were red with a red piping. The cuffs were slashed and it is uncertain from contemporary illustrations if these were red or blue. They were ornamented with three brass buttons. The waistcoat was white. The breeches were white in summer and blue in winter. In both orders of dress black buttoned gaiters were worn over the black shoes. Some contemporary illustrations depict a waist-belt with a brass buckle ornamented with a anchor design.

The cross belts held a black ammunition pouch on the right hip and a short brass hilted sword and the bayonet on the left side.

The naval artillery undress uniform was similar to that of the naval infantry, the main difference was in the cuff ornamentation.

The artillery cap was of blue woollen material piped in red with a tassel falling down on the left side. The short jacket was blue with a stand and fall

78 *(Below right)* Naval infantry in full dress (*c.* 1805)

77 (*Below*) Naval artillery in undress (*c.* 1805)

collar, the lapels were fastened back each side by a row of seven brass buttons. There is no definate information as to the colour of the lapels but it probably was red as this was in fact the lining of the jacket. The cuffs were the same pattern as for the full dress coat, red with a red slash, fastened with three brass buttons. The trousers were three-quarter length and worn without shoes or stockings when at sea, but with the white stockings and shoes on other occasions.

Naval infantry 1805

The battalions of naval infantry at Trafalgar were dressed in a short blue coat with lapels and a standing collar. The coat was double breasted with seven brass buttons in each row, the top button fastened back the lapel. The collar was ornamented with an anchor in gold. The cuffs were red and decorated with three brass buttons. A white waistcoat was worn in this order of dress, fastened by a row of brass buttons. Blue breeches and black half boots, a short sword with a brass hilt was worn on the left hip. This uniform was similar to the Spanish naval artillery. The hat was a bicorne in black felt but with a red pompom instead of a plume as worn by the naval artillery.

The undress uniform for naval infantry consisted of a short jacket of blue cloth with lapels and a standing collar, with two rows of seven brass buttons. The cuffs were red with long yellow lace button holes, half on the cuff and the other half on the sleeve itself. The trousers were blue worn loose

79 (*Below left*) Naval artillery in summer uniform (*c.* 1805)

80 (*Below*) Naval artillery in winter uniform (*c.* 1805)

at the calf without shoes or stockings when at sea, but in port or on land white stockings, black buckled shoes was customary. The cap was of blue cloth, a tasseled bag hanging down at the left hand side. This cap was piped in red with a red tassel. At the front of the cap was a badge depicting the crown and anchor. A flintlock musket was carried in full dress with black cross belts to support the ammunition pouch to the bayonet.

Sailors 1805

Spanish crew members were dressed in various degrees of uniformity. Regulations of 1793 laid down that each sailor 'had to bring at least three shirts, two long woollen trousers made of Retine or of striped linen according to the Climate of the Voyage. Two pairs of woollen or linen socks, one pair of shoes, two waistcoats, one long jacket, one cap and one short jacket to protect them from the cold and inclement weather when he is working.'

In these regulations there is no mention of colour, however, the shirts were white, the trousers dark blue cloth or striped white linen. They wore Catalonian caps of blue material, the tops falling to the left or right. The jacket was also blue with a falling collar, single breasted and fastened by a row of eight brass buttons. A sash and neckerchief complete the costume. Shoes and socks were usually only worn in port or on shore.

In action the coat was discarded and they would fight in their shirts or stripped to the waist, the neckerchief was worn around the head and over the ears, firstly to keep the sweat out of the eyes and secondly to protect the eardrums from the deafening crash of the guns firing in a very confined space.

There were no naval regulations for crew members until 1840. The amount of uniformity depended greatly on the ship's captain and more often than not the depth of his purse.

The round hat in black pitch or straw was not used in the Spanish navy until 1833.

The 1793 Regulations describe the uniform for boatswains and mates as 'a blue jacket with lapels, blue waistcoat and long trousers. Red cuffs to the sleeves. Brass buttons engraved with an anchor. Cocked hat without any lace and a red silk cockade. The first boatswains to have their waistcoats edged with gold lace. The second boatswain and mates to have their waistcoat pocket flaps edged in gold lace only'.

Spanish officers' swords at Trafalgar

The sword of Admiral Don Frederico Gravina whose flagship was the *Principe de Asturias*, is now to be seen at the Museo Naval in Madrid. The hilt is of solid gilded brass with a square grip, there is fluting down the front and back of the oval pommel, and the knuckle bow and quillion are plain. The blade is straight and flattened oval section and the scabbard is of black fishskin with gilt mountings. This small sword was introduced in 1717 when naval regulations first appeared for the Spanish navy – one of the first countries to do so. The small sword is based on that of the Spanish guard regiment which had a silver hilt and to make the distinction the naval sword was ordered to be of gilt brass. This type of sword was, of course, not regarded as a purely fighting weapon and a more suitable weapon for ship-to-ship fighting was devised. The Naval Museum at Madrid has in its collection two swords of this type and date; one is based on the British light cavalry sword introduced in 1796 with a brass stirrup hilt and the grip bound in wire. The black leather scabbard has two brass lockets with rings and a chape. The other is based on the French light cavalry sword of that time described in the French section (p. 68). At the centre of the quillions there is a rectangular plaque decorated with an embossed anchor superimposed on a trophy of flags. The black leather scabbard has gilt brass mountings, with hooks for frog attachment. The sword of Don Francisco Riquelme, an officer aboard the flag ship *Santa Ana* was surrendered to Vice-Admiral Sir Cuthbert Collingwood at Trafalgar. The hilt of this sword is of the slotted pattern, used in the British Royal Navy from about 1770. The pommel is fashioned as a lion's head and the metal guard has two parallel slots cut in the curve of the knuckle-bow along the crosspiece, one each side of the blade. The blade is engraved 'real fabrica de toledo ano 1797'. All the mountings are gilt.

The design of a dress sword dated 10 August 1802 in the Museo Naval, Madrid, has a polygonal grip, larger in the centre. The pommel is in the form of the royal crown, the knuckle bow is in the form of a piece of rope and the quillions have scrolled finials and at their centre is a circular plaque bearing within a circlet of beads two crossed anchors with the crown above.

Cutlasses in the Spanish navy followed the British pattern through to the 1850s.

Dirks were worn by Spanish midshipmen and were of no particular pattern the only uniformity being the use of an anchor as decoration on the blade or hilt. Ivory or mother-of-pearl grips were popular, as were eagle or lion's-head pommels. Scabbards were of black leather with gilt brass mountings or entirely of gilt brass.

The sword of Rear Admiral Don Ballaga Hidalgo Cisneros, now in the Nelson collection at Monmouth, England has an urn-shaped pommel with grips and quillions decorated with intertwined beads. The flat shell is pieced with an intertwined pattern as is the grip. The triangular hollow-ground blade is now rusted into the scabbard. The rear admiral was wounded aboard the *Santissima Trinidad* his flagship, which was totally dismasted and later sunk.

Weapons of the ship's company

Hand-to-hand fighting was done with boarding pikes, cutlasses, axes and muskets. The boarding pike had a steel point and a wooden shaft six foot long. Its main used was to prod boarders off the sides of the ship. The cutlass was a small weapon with a curved blade. Ideal for the cramped close quarters of deck fighting. These weapons were kept under the supervision of the Master at Arms and were held in fittings around the masts. Dirks would be used by the midshipmen. The pistols were usually plain and with the ramrod in a stirrup to prevent it being dropped or lost, they also had a spring hook on the side to allow the weapon to be held in a belt. The muskets were similar to army issue, the only difference being the use of a wooden ram-rod in place of steel, since they had the advantage of not suffering from corrosion at sea. A brass cap was not placed on the fore end of the wood, the reason being that bayonets were not used in the navy and therefore in the interest of economy, the protective brass cap was dispensed with. There was little change in the design of the sea service musket after 1800 until the end of the flintlock era.

The musketoon, which was a member of the blunderbuss family, had a bore of about one and one half inches, with a muzzle of two and one half inches. These weapons fired a heavy charge of shot and were used for repelling boarders. Their weight of eighteen pounds average, required the use of a rest which fitted into the ship's rail. Another weapon was the seven barrelled volley gun. These weapons had a 45 bore and were made with six barrels surrounding the centre one. These were not popular because of the weight and difficulty of reloading. Lord Nelson did not approve of musket fire from the masts of his ships because of the danger of setting fire to the vessel and it is ironic that his death was caused by one of these sharpshooters, popular in the French navy.

Tomahawks or battle-axes were also used as weapons but could be useful in cutting away broken spars, and grappeling irons. These were kept with the boarding pikes around the masts. Pistols were used sometimes, the difference for sea service would usually only be a belt hook so that both hands may be free for a cutlass and for moving from ship to ship.

The French and Spanish navies used the same weapons as the British. The French relied heavily on men armed with muskets up in the rigging to shoot the deck crew of the opposing ship and put out of action all the deck guns. The French and Spanish also used boarding pikes. The French pattern having a broader blade. Cutlasses and pistols were also standard ship equipment.

Glossary

Admiral

This word may be traced from the arabic *amir-al-bahr*, which means 'commander of the seas'. The Romans called their admirals *sarraccenorum admiral* inserting the letter 'd' into the latin form. The term was found in the Venetian and Genoese navies and was brought to Great Britain from the East by the Crusaders. In 1297 Edward I created William de Leybown the first English admiral under the title, 'Admiral of the sea of the King of England'. The title carried with it great power and was eventually incorporated into the office of Lord High Admiral of England. The first commission of an admiral was in 1302, and appointed Gervase Aland, Captain and Admiral. The title Admiral delegated legal powers and the captain delegated executive command. In the reign of Edward III the chief naval officer was known as Custos Maris guardian of the sea and the early English form of the word was Amiral or Ammiral, the latter form being used by Milton, Cromwell's secretary of state. The present spelling of the word probably arose from the belief that it was an abridged form of admirable or that it was a compound with the Latin AD. The office of Lord High Admiral was created by Henry IV in 1405 and survived with breaks until 1828 when its administrative functions were vested into the board of admiralty. These powers had been of great importance and carried with it certain judicial functions which since 1875 have been vested in the admiralty division of the high court.

The first Lord High Admiral was the Earl of Somerset and from his time onwards the duties were exercised by an individual until 1632 when for the first time the office was put into commission, all the great officers of state being commissioners. During the Commonwealth naval officers were at first directed by parliament, but later Cromwell took control himself. When Charles II was restored he appointed his brother James to be Lord High Admiral. After the revolution of 1688, the office was again put into commission, in which position it has remained to date except for three years. In 1707–09 when the title was held by the consort of Queen Anne, and in 1827–28 when William IV was Lord High Admiral.

Louis XIV introduced the title of Admiral into the French Navy, the rank was equivalent to that of Marshal of France, but the holders became so powerful that Cardinal Richelieu suppressed it and assumed the office himself. Unfortunately many of these appointed used the title to enrich themselves, when one holder relinquished the title in 1759 he was awarded an annual pension of some £6000 which was held by his family until the outbreak of the French Revolution. In February 1805 Napoleon appointed Marshal Murat, his brother-in-law.

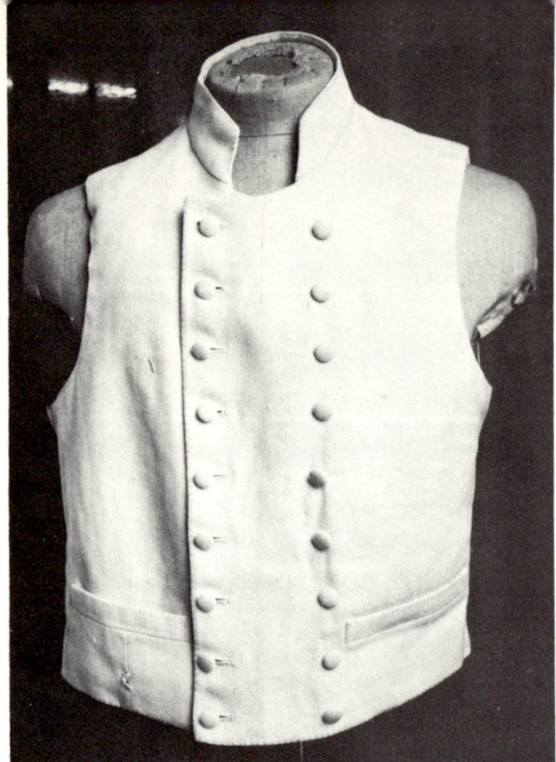

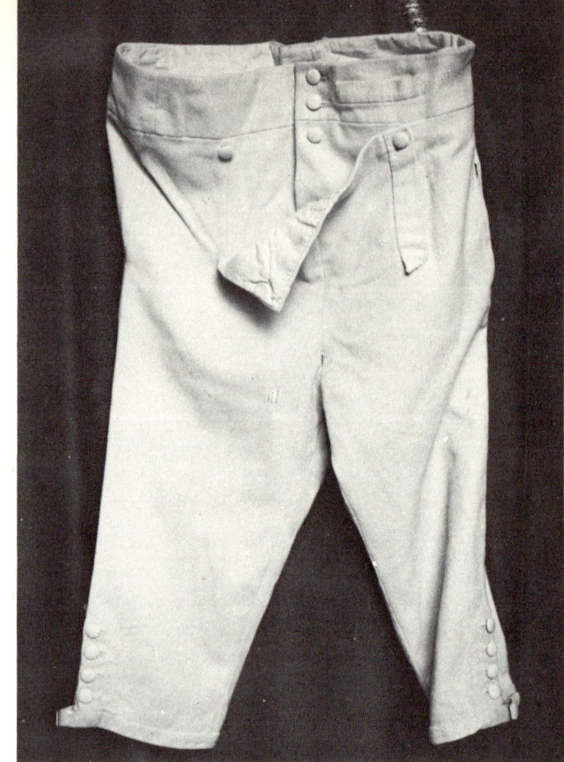

81 *(Above)* Double-breasted pattern waistcoat (Nelson wore a civilian pattern at Trafalgar) (*c.* 1805)

82 *(Above right)* Officer's breeches (*c.* 1805)

Admiral, vice-
This title evolved from that of the lieutenant-admiral, an office which fulfilled the duties of secretary and assistant to the admiral. Later the office was known as vice-admiral from 1672, and as vice-admiral of Great Britain in 1717. The office lapsed after the Napoleonic era, until 1901 when Edward VII revived the rank.

Admiral, rear-
This was the rank of Lord Nelson at the battle of Trafalgar and had been instituted by Charles II for his natural son the Duke of Grafton so that he might have a title. Nelson had waited 18 years for his flag rank, but was still under 40 years old when he received it.

Aiguillette
A twisted gold or silver cord worn suspended from the left or right shoulder to denote a particular officer or appointment. Naval aiguillettes are usually made with a navy-blue silk thread running through as opposed to the army pattern which have red. The aiguillette was not used in the British navy at the time of Trafalgar but was more common on the continent of Europe and could be seen on the uniforms of the newly created French navy resurrected after the Revolution and also on the uniforms of the Spanish navy, where it was used as a sign of rank, by midshipmen, fastened to their right shoulder from a twisted gold shoulder cord.

Aide-de-camp
A phrase used to denote an officer of the staff who passes on the orders of the Commander.

Badge
Devised to show rank or position and could be made in metal, die-struck, or embroidered in silk or gold wire. More commonly used in the French and Spanish navies at the time of Trafalgar.

Blue cloth
The material used for naval uniforms, this had been the common colour for all

navies from before Trafalgar and since that date to the present. Presumably the colour denotes the sea and is also easy to dye. In difficult circumstances dark blue is the most suitable colour to manufacture.

Blue jacket

The name given to lower-deck ratings in common parlance. Derived from the blue-cloth jacket but was worn by crew members, especially on formal occasions. The degree of the use of jacket was to an extent according to the captain's purse. At the time of Trafalgar it was unofficial.

Boatswain

The Saxon word 'swein' meant a servant, boat swein referred to the servant of the boat. In those days a boat meant a ship and not the small boats carried in her. The word coxswain is similarly derived for cock is an old word for a smaller type of rowing boat. A boatswain is a commissioned officer in the Royal Navy and is responsible for all rigging, cordage, anchors, sails and boats, to keep them in a state of good repair and to make reports on their number and condition. By means of his whistle, which became his badge of office, he summoned the crew to their duties. He shared in the work of the ship and took a place in one of the watches. He himself gives no orders, but acts as the officer to the first lieutenant.

Bonnet

A soft cap or covering for the head and without a brim, used by ships crews of all nations before the introduction of a regulation headdress. This could be pulled down over the ears in heavy weather and when aloft in the rigging. It also protected the ears from the noise of cannon fire. In between decks, the fear of deafness was a reality due to the confined and enclosed space.

Braid

Common and incorrect term for lace which ornamented an officer's uniform and denoted his rank. Braid is in fact a wool or silk cord and is usually applied to the lower ranks' uniforms as decoration and a sign of non-commissioned rank.

Branch Officer

An officer who holds a specific or specialized employment within a ship. boatswain, master-at-arms, chief gunner. In more modern days these became commissioned rank officers.

Breeches

Nether garments to cover the legs. In naval terms these would have been close fitting breeches or pantaloons made of woollen material or stocking-net in white or blue. For use on formal occasions white was the regulation colour, and Lord Nelson was seen in no other garment. The breeches were fastened at the knee with buckles and were worn with white stockings or were also made to come half way down the calf and worn with gaiters. This latter mode was adopted by the Spanish naval artillery and can be seen in illustration 80. They could also be worn with leather boots, which was a fashion among the junior or younger officers of all the navies.

Buckle

The mode of fastening shoes of the Trafalgar period made of brass or gilt brass. They could also be made of silver gilt. This style of shoe disappeared from the officers wardrobe about 1827 when they were only required to be worn with white breeches and stockings at court.

Button

Usually made of brass and in gilt brass for officers' uniforms. In the Trafalgar period most buttons were engraved and not die-struck. In 1800 button makers' names were first stamped on the backs of buttons. Before this date buttons were usually flat and in one piece, but these were slowly replaced by others of slightly convex form. As the convexity of the face increased the back was filled.

Some tailors had their names stamped on buttons but this was only if they were ordered in great quantities. Tailors tended to buy the buttons as required when the uniform was made. There were many manufacturers in London and Birmingham. In addition, the manufacturer usually made other metal fittings for uniforms and in some cases sold gold and silver lace and embroidery for uniforms. Some companies are still button makers dating back to Trafalgar and before, such as Firmin and Sons who can trace their history back to 1677, and the firm of Jennens and Co. who amalgamated with J. R. Gaunt & Sons, date back to 1800. Other manufacturers who have now disappeared or who have been amalgamated include Hammond, Turner & Sons dating from 1717; Edward Armfield, founded in 1763; Charles Pitt & Co.; Sclater & Sons, J. Stewart & John Johnston, both of Edinburgh; Herbert & Co., W. Twiss & Co.; Lambert & Co., and Prosser of London and Birmingham.

In France and Spain buttons were manufactured in the same manner and officers' buttons were fitted by the tailor who had them made to order for him. Although the French Revolution had ruined the business of these tradesmen, the advent of Empire had revived them to an even greater degree.

Caps

A covering for the head and in a naval context usually with a peak. These caps did not appear in the British navy until about 1815 when the officers of the ship *Phaeton* adopted them. The Prince Regent approved and ordered that his yacht crew should be similarly supplied. In France and Spain the men were supplied with caps. The French style was similar to a side cap, popular in the last war. The Spanish pattern had a loose top which fell to the shoulder and was ornamented with a tassel. The French marine cap was decorated with a gold anchor on the front and a binding of gold lace.

Captain

Title found in most languages to denote a chief of a small band of men and comes from the Latin *caput*, head or chief. Strictly the commanding officer of a man-of-war or of a frigate carrying at least 20 cannons. Captain is next in rank to the rear admiral or commodore. This rank was first clearly defined in the British navy in 1748 and divided the captain into three grades. It was decided that any officer in command was entitled to the rank of captain while

83 Vice admiral's hat with the famous 'Chilingk' plume

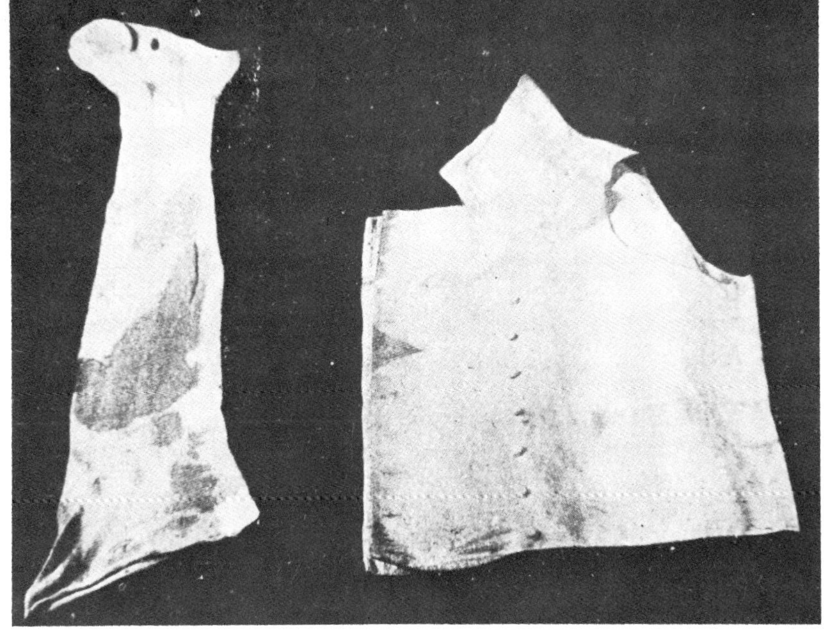

84 Waistcoat and stocking worn by Nelson at Trafalgar (note blood stains)

in command, regardless of his present rank. All captains eligible for promotion to rear admirals were originally known as masters and commanders; in 1794 the word master was omitted. Post captain was a term used to distinguish captains commanding frigates from commanders next in rank. There was never a commission of post captain, the term arose from the fact that these officers' names were posted in a book as ready for promotion. Captains, if of three years standing ranked with colonels in the army. He is responsible for military government, navigation, and equipment of his ship, for the crews discipline and health, and for neglect of duties by his inferior officers. A flag captain, commands the admiral's ship. The captain of the fleet is a temporary official appointed by the admiralty to keep up the discipline of the fleet. He acts under the commander in chief as adjutant general of the force and wears the uniform of rear admiral.

The title captain was also given to the chief sailor of particular sections of the crew, in charge of certain portions of the ship's company – such as 'captain of the top', 'captain of the gun', 'captain of the hold'.

Chevron

Braid used to denote a non-commissioned rank and in some countries the length of service. Usually made of a woven tape in various colours.

Cloak

Known in the navy as a boat cloak and had been worn since the eighteenth century but did not receive official recognition until the Dress Regulations of 1891. They were used when travelling in a small boat from ship to ship. In the Trafalgar period there was no set pattern except that they should be blue and lined blue. They usually had a stand-and-fall collar and fastened with brass lion heads and a chain. They protected the body from the sea and weather, and allowed one to clamber up a ship's side more easily than a coat.

Cockade

Rosette worn on a hat usually to display the national colours, often made of pleated wool or silk, sometimes painted metal. The Spanish cockade was red at the time of Trafalgar. The French, red, white and blue. In the British service colours were not used and the cockade was usually black pleated wool or silk.

Cocked hat

Broad brimmed hat turned up each side and known as a bicorne (or if turned up on three sides, a tricorne). Usually made of black felt or beaver and bound with a silk edge, sometimes gold lace. The tricorne was worn with the angle to the front where a bicorne was worn athwartships by flag officers and fore-and-aft by other officers. In the Spanish navy all the officers wore the hat athwartships, while in the French navy officers wore them fore-and-aft.

Commander

Title given to the captain of the second rank in the British Royal Navy. A commander is generally given the command of a small vessel. The responsibility of navigation is usually given to this officer. It was introduced to the navy by William III. Commanders were appointed second in command in the dress regulations of 1827.

Cook

In the days of the navy of sail this post was given to a sailor who was disabled or past climbing the rigging. The perquisites were good and 'Captains of Tops', 'Old Quartermasters', etc. looked forward to the post. Although it was decreeed that all cooks must have two arms, many had only one good leg.

Cord

Decoration for uniform of woven material in the round, used for piping seams on jackets.

Counter epaulette

An epaulette without fringes.

Cravat

Cloth worn round neck and displayed in the open collar. This was gradually disappearing at the time of Trafalgar, as the collars became closed.

Crest

The comb on top of a head-dress.

Cut of his jib

In the days of sail, a ship could often be distinguished by her sails. Especially her jibs. French ships often had two jibs, Spanish ships had a small jib or none at all. This could also apply to other sailors. Thus, the phrase was often associated with uniform: 'By the cut of his jib he's a Frenchman'.

Distinction lace

The gold lace on officers' uniforms determining rank usually by width or amount used.

Dimity

A linen cloth of an open weave, often made with a fine blue line running through. Popular as a summer wear material.

Ditty box

A small box carried by sailors in which they keep their needles, thread, wool and cloth, originally they were kept in a bag made of 'dittis' or Manchester cloth, hence the name 'ditty box'.

Embroidery

System of decorating a uniform with gold wire, usually for higher ranking officers. Most of the wires used are hollow and allow a needle and thread to be passed through them, the wire is cut to the required length and laid down on the garment, the pattern having already been applied with a stencil. Used a great deal in the French and Spanish navies, but little in the British navy, where the officers' uniforms were ornamented with gold lace rather than embroidery, the epaulettes being the exception. Lord Nelson's decorations were embroidered direct onto the undress coat he wore at Trafalgar.

Ensign

An ensign was a young officer in the French army and was later introduced into the French navy as a commissioned rank. It was not used in the British

Royal Navy, a sub-lieutenant being the equivalent.

Epaulette

A shoulder strap with a fringed end lined and padded with red or blue cloth (later changed to silk) used to denote a commissioned rank. At the time of Trafalgar these were fairly simple in design, the strap was of gold lace, pointed at the shoulder and sewn with a button hole so that it could be attached to the shoulder. The fringe was made of bullion gold wire, that is gold wire pulled and twisted on itself so that it becomes twice as large. These were sewn onto the end with one bullion sewn on the strap in a crescent to hide the joins. Stars denoted the ranks in both the French and British navies.

Admiral – two gold epaulettes each having three silver stars.

Vice-admiral – two gold epaulettes each having two silver stars.

Rear-admiral – two gold epaulettes each having one silver star.

Captain of three or more years in that post – two plain gold epaulettes.

Captain of less than three years standing – one plain gold epaulette on the right shoulder.

Commander – one plain gold epaulette on the left shoulder.

On the undress uniform officers of flag rank always wore them whereas for officers below that rank it was optional.

Spanish naval officers did not wear epaulettes at this time.

Facings

The collar, cuffs, turnbacks and plastrons of a uniform are usually of a different colour to the rest of the coat, and are called facings.

Flag Officer

The ranks above that of captain, that is rear-admiral, vice-admiral and admiral. He is so called because he is privileged to hoist a flag at his mast-head instead of a pennon. The flag being a red St. George's cross on a white ground. A rear admiral carries it at the mizzen, a vice admiral at the fore, and an admiral at the main. They are appointed by the admiralty at the sovereign's pleasure.

Frock

The sleeved shirt worn by sailors and crewmen, in various colours at the whim of the captains, who would pay for them out of his own purse, if he wanted a uniform crew.

Foul anchor

An anchor fouled by a cable or chain, and used as the design on officers' buttons in the navy. Also used as a badge for collars in the Spanish navy. The French used the design on buttons and caps.

Full dress

Uniform worn on formal occasions onboard, or worn going ashore, visiting the admiralty or court, visits abroad or to other foreign ships.

Galon

Width of lace used to decorate a hat and hide the fastening that held the plume.

Gorget

Originally a piece of armour worn around the neck. When the wearing of armour fell into disuse the gorget continued to be worn by officers as a badge of rank when on duty. It was a half-moon plate suspended from the collar by two ribbons, made of silver or silver gilt. The Royal Marine officers' gorgets were silver-gilt and engraved with the royal coat of arms, below in a shield was engraved a fouled anchor surrounded by a spray of laurels.

Gloves

White gloves were worn with full dress on ceremonial occasions, whilst black gloves were prescribed for funerals.

Hessian boots
Knee boots with knotched fronts popular with cavalry, but also found their way in the navy of this period. Fashionable in civilian life, they were usually worn by the younger officers. The Duke of Clarence when Lord High Admiral tried to have them officially recognized without success. When going into action Vice Admiral Collingwood noted that one of the younger officers was wearing Hessian boots, he advised him to go below and change into breeches and stockings as these would 'be so much more manageable for the surgeon'.
Hose
Stockings, usually woollen, although sometimes of silk or worsted, to be worn with breeches. A midshipman when joining his ship would include amongst his personal clothing six pairs of wool, six pairs of worsted and two pairs of silk stockings.
Jacket
Upper garment with sleeves, fastened with buttons across the chest. The French, Spanish and British navies all had crew members wearing Jackets, usually blue cloth with brass buttons, piped with cord or tape along the seams for decoration.
Lace
Invariably called braid, but officially lace, and known by the manufacturers by this name. It is gold or silver wire woven onto a silk base by a shuttle. Made in any widths up to four inches wide. In the days of Nelson it was made by hand. The gold wire used has to be of the highest quality because of the danger of tarnishing at sea and consequently the cost was (and still is) high for sea services. Various designs could be woven into the lace; for example, the pattern for flag officers and used on Lord Nelson's coat was called vellum and check. But many manufacturers had their own name for the patterns which they used amongst themselves and the tailors who bought the lace from them to use on the uniforms.

France had, and to a great extent still has, a flourishing business in gold lace and embroidery. In Spain too the trade has been kept alive, particularly by the Church.
Lapel
The turnback on a coat, usually of the facing colour and fastened back onto the buttons.
Lieutenant
Devised from the French word *lieu* which means 'in place of'. He is the subordinate of the captain, but able to assume command if the captain were disabled. A ship of the line in Nelson's time could carry as many as eight, smaller ships one or more. The first lieutenant was responsible for the running of the ship, and did the executive work; the second lieutenant was in charge of gunnery.
'Make and mend'
In the Royal Navy, an afternoon, usually Thursday, when the men are piped on deck to make and mend clothes. Captain John Boteler described how his ship's company set about making their clothes:

> They were issued with twelve yards of duck, thread and needles and a black silk hankerchief. A brass nail was driven in the deck at three or six yard intervals as a guide for measuring. They would run to the galley, burn a stick, down on the deck, dot off the shape and commence work at once. Others, unable to do this, would give their grog to those more

expert, and the consequence was, at the end of only one week, there were not above fifty without a suit. The same thing with straw hats. Every bum boat was expected to bring off a bundle of peculiar grass, and soon you would see men at their work at their sennet and in a very short time with first rate hats.

Captain Boteler's recollections edited by David Bonner Smith, Naval Records Society

Marines
Soldiers on a ship to back up the authority of the captain in the days of pressed seamen and used in a similar manner in the French and Spanish navies. The British Royal Marines fought in great number during the Napoleonic Wars and at Trafalgar. Some 92 officers and 2600 men served at the battle of whom four officers and 113 men were killed and more than 200 wounded. French marines were included in the Imperial Guard and as such were regarded as superior troops.

Master
An officer who ranks above a lieutenant and who navigates the ship under the direction of the captain. Highest rank by warrant and also taught the midshipmen.

Master-at-arms
This office evolved from that of the ship's corporal and was introduced to the British navy by Charles II. The master-at-arms was in charge of the discipline of the ship and exercised the ship's company with cutlass and musket and made sure all weapons were in good repair and working order. He was by rank a first class petty officer.

Mate
Term applied to any seaman who was assistant or deputy in any work such as gunner's mate or boatswain's mate. In the British Royal Navy the rank was that of a non-commissioned officer but not in line for promotion.

Midshipmen
These were young gentlemen, put by their parents under the care and patronage of a captain to learn the profession of seaman. They ranked junior to master's mates. By going to sea this was the only way that they could learn and hope to pass their examination to a lieutenancy. The midshipmen could be incredibly young. Lord Nelson was himself only twelve when he first joined his ship.

Nankeen
A very fine linen cloth, usually expensive and used for summer wear clothing. Brought from China originally.

National Blue
Used by the French to describe the colour navy blue. The most popular colour in the French Revolution and part of the National colours. The complete French forces were dressed in national blue except for some cavalry units and the Swiss regiments.

Paymaster
Officer of a ship's company who keeps the accounts and is in charge of provisions. He was of warrant officer rank but did not receive a full dress uniform until 1807, two years after Trafalgar.

Pouch
Leather box to hold ammunition or powder usually suspended from a leather belt over the shoulder.

85 Jewel of the Sardinian Order of St Joachim (worn by Nelson)

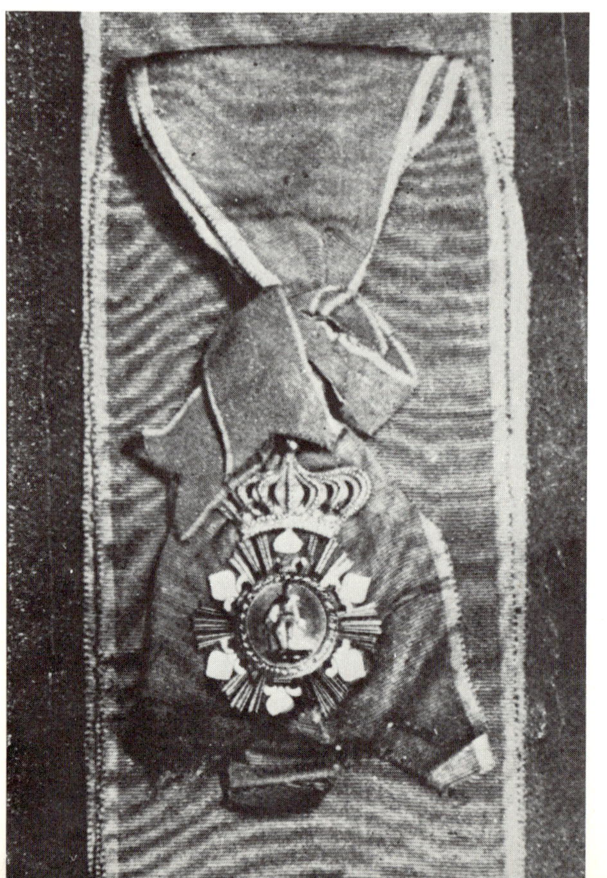

86 *(Above left)* Gold Star of the Turkish Order of the Crescent (worn by Nelson)

87 *(Above)* Badge of the Order of the Crescent and Cross of St Joachim (worn by Nelson)

88 *(Left)* Grand Cross of the Neapolitan Order of San Ferdinando (worn by Nelson)

Pigtail
Pigtail or queue. Hair worn pulled back into a tail and tied with a ribbon, a fashion that was gradually disappearing at the time of Trafalgar and was not seem after about 1820. In 1805 a sailor on the *Royal Sovereign* was described as 'Having a pigtail down to his sternpost'.
Quartermaster
Originally this rating was assigned to duties looking after the troops quarters but after troops ceased to be carried other duties were assigned to these men such as steering the ship.
Russia Braid
A flat cord woven onto a silk base in gold or silver. Because of the way the material is made it may look as though it is two cords joined together. 1/32-in wide.
Sailor
From the old English word 'saylor'. Generally speaking, sailor refers to one before the mast.
Sash
Length of fringed netted silk worn around the waist and usually denotes officer rank. Not worn in the British Royal navy except by Royal Marine officers whose dress followed army dictates. In the French navy sashes were worn by flag officers, in various colours to denote flag rank.
Admirals – Gold and white netted silk with two tassels.
Vice admiral – Gold and scarlet netted silk.
Rear admiral – Gold and sky blue.
Shoes
Officers wore buckled shoes with orders of dress requiring breeches and stockings. The crew members wore shoes only in port or when on shore. Bare feet helped for a better hold on deck and in the rigging.
Slops
Originally 'sloppe', which was a type of breeches, but became a general term for ready-made clothes issues onboard to seamen.
Straw hat
Straw hats were mostly imported from the West Indies and could be covered in brown holland and painted black. It was then painted with the name of the ship or some nautical decoration.
Stock
Cloth worn around the neck made of a black material, later of leather and fitted to the inside of the collar, discontinued about 1830.
Sword belt
Made of leather and often embroidered on the outer edge in gold wire before the belt was assembled, with a gilt buckle and gilt fittings. Worn over the trousers or breeches. In the British and Spanish navies the sword belt was usually worn under the waistcoat and so made of a strong tape lined with leather, only the slings or the frog-fitting showing outside, these could be of blue leather and ornamented in the same manner as the belt worn over the trousers or breeches.
Sword knot
In the shock of combat a sword or cutlass could easily be knocked from the hand and into the sea, therefore the purpose of a sword knot was to attach the sword to the users wrist so that even if it was knocked out of his hand he could still retrieve it. British officers' naval sword knot was made of a length of uniform lace ending in a bullion tassel. Embroidered on the top of the tassel was a fouled anchor. In France the admirals' sword knot had a strap of oak-leaf

lace, the top of the tassel was ornamented with silver stars to denote the flag rank. Officers below this rank used a plain gold strap and knot.

Surgeon

Since 1787 surgeons had been dressed as warrant officers, but in 1805 they were recognized as officers and dressed as such, but 'to be subordinate in rank to the lieutenants of the ships that they might be employed'. Even on the largest ship of the line there would be only one surgeon, who would be assisted by hospital mates. The difficulties of surgery were enormous, carried on as they were in the bowels of the ship, heaving from side to side, with only a candle to work by.

Trousers

Not generally worn in the British navy at the time of Trafalgar by the officers, only by the seamen. In white or blue and white stripes. When Captain John Boteler presented himself at the admiralty wearing a full dress coat and white jean trousers, he was politely told to go away and come back in breeches and stockings. In the Spanish and French navies the same applied and trousers were to be seen only among crew members.

Turnbacks

That part of the coat at the waist which was turned back and buttoned behind, originally when coats were long they were buttoned back to allow free movement but gradually the coat got shorter and so did the turnbacks until they were dispensed with altogether and the coat became a round jacket.

Undress

Uniform worn on informal occasions and generally when at sea, also worn in action. This uniform was worn by Lord Nelson at Trafalgar.

Waistcoat

Sleeveless coat worn under the jacket, single breasted and fastened by a row of brass buttons. Pockets with or without flaps. In the British service they were plain white and without ornamentation. French flag officers' waistcoats were heavily embroidered according to rank. In the Spanish navy they were edged in gold lace.

Appendix A

Naval outfitters, embroiderers, hatters and button manufacturers, 1805

London		
Thomas Allen	18 Old Bond Street	Tailors
Amery & Pitter	26 Bedford Street	Gold lacemen
Barret, Corney & Corney	479 Strand	Gold lacemen & embroiderers
William & George Bicknell	1 Old Bond Street	Hatters, hosiers & glovers
Bodley & Etty	31 Lombard Street	Gold lacemen & embroiderers
John Alexander Cater & Sons	67 Pall Mall	Hatters & accoutrement manufacturers
Joseph Cator	58 Bishops gate	Hatters
Joseph Dean	2 Craven Street, Strand	Gold & silver lacemen
James John & Joseph Esdale	110 Bunhill Row	Accoutrement manufacturers
Firmin & Westall	153 Strand	Button manufacturers
Thomas Hawkes	24 Piccadilly	Hat & Cap maker & accoutrement manufacturers
James Lawson	181 Strand	Hatter
James Lock	6 St James's Street	Hatter
Thomas Lonsdale & Son	32 King Street, Covent Garden	Gold & silver lacemen
Robert Loxham	88 Cornhill	Hatter
J. & B. Odell	85 New Bond Street	Hatter, Gold & Silver lacemen
William & Charles Prater	7 Charing Cross	Tailors & accoutrement manufacturers
Richard Thresher	152 Strand	Hosier
Charles Webb	57 Piccadilly	Gold & silver lacemen
Welch & Stalker	134 Leadenhall Street	Slopsellers & Merchants
J. W. Yardley	5 Thorney Street	Buckle makers
Edinburgh		
George Hunter	12 Parliament Street	Merchant and contractor
Winchester		
John Flight	St Thomas Street	Tailor and breeches manufacturer

London tailors established premises on the south coast such as Portsmouth, Plymouth and Southsea in the middle of the last century. The most famous perhaps, of all naval outfitters, Messrs Gieves Ltd., were not established until 1863.

Nelson bought his cocked hats at James Lock, the hatter in St James's Street. The hat he wore at Trafalgar was purchased, according to this famous hatter's accounts on the 20 August 1805. Fitted with a cockade and an eye shade to cover his right eye. He ordered a second hat four days later. On the 14 September he called for the last time, collected his cocked hats and settled his account – £1. 15. 0 – and left for Portsmouth. One of the James Lock hats, complete with the eye shade, can be seen on the wax effigy at Westminster Abbey.

In the Nelson Museum, Monmouth, is an interesting invoice from Barrett, Corney and Corney to Lord Nelson for the gold-embroidered decorations that the company supplied between 1803–05. These were the four orders of knighthood: the Order of the Bath, St Ferdinand, St Joachim and the Crescent. These decorations and the coat can be seen in illustrations and also at the National Maritime Museum, Greenwich. Pasted on the back of the Barrett, Corney and Corney invoice on a separate piece of paper are some instructions regarding Lord Nelson's coat sleeve, the pocket and sword knot of his undress coat. The sword knot is of the 1805 pattern and presumably Nelson required the new type before leaving on his next voyage. The account was settled by his Lordship, at a cost of £21. 12. od. on the 7 September 1805.

John Salter of 35 Strand, London was Nelson's sword cutler and in 1802 he left the hat he wore at the battle of Copenhagen, at these premises. This was presented in 1948 to the Royal United Services Institute Museum, Whitehall.

Bibliography

Knotel & Seig, *Handbuch der Uniformkunde*, Hamburg 1937

Dudley Jarrett, *British Naval Dress*, J.M. Dent 1960

Professor M. Lewis, C.B.E., F.S.A., *England's Sea Officers*

H. Malibran, *Des Uniforms de L'Armée Français*, Paris 1902

John Mollo, *Uniforms of the Royal Navy during the Napoleonic Wars*, Hugh Evelyn Ltd. 1965

Commander B. Campbell, *Customs & Traditions of the Royal Navy*, Gale & Polden Ltd. 1956

Dudley Pope, *England Expects*, Weidenfeld & Nicolson 1959

Tom Pocock, *Nelson and his World*, Thames & Hudson 1968

Arthur Bryant, *Nelson*, Collins 1970

J. Wilkinson Latham, *British Cut & Thrust Weapons*, David & Charles 1971

Oliver Warner, *Great Sea Battles*, Weidenfeld & Nicolson 1963

P.C. Smith, *Per mare per terram. A History of the Royal Marines*, Balfour 1974

Colonel C. Field, *Britain's Sea Soldiers*, Vols. 1 & 2, Lyceum Press 1924

Commander W.E. May R.N., *The dress of naval officers*, National Maritime Museum 1966

Admiral Sir Gerald Dickens, *The Dress of the British Sailor*, National Martime Museum 1957

Michael Lewis, *A Social History of the Navy 1793–1815*, Hodder & Stoughton 1960

Claude Farrere, *Histoire de la Marine Française*, Flammarion 1962

Peter Kemp, *History of the Royal Navy*, Arthur Baker 1969

Philip Warner, *Life in Nelson's Navy*

Geoffrey Bennett, *The Battle of Trafalgar*, Batsford 1977

Index

Admiral
British: 17, 18, 19, 20, 21, 22, 23, 25, 35, 38, 39, 41, 68, 81, 82, 84, 85, 87, 88, 91; French: 10, 42, 43, 46, 47, 52, 68, 69, 71; Spanish: 72, 73, 74, 78, 79
Anchor 19, 24, 27, 28, 30, 31, 32, 33, 35, 36, 39, 40, 43, 47, 58, 68, 69, 71, 75, 76, 77, 78, 79, 83, 84, 87, 91

Boatswain 11, 12, 14, 15, 33, 61, 78, 83, 89
Boots 21, 26, 29, 43, 46, 50, 75, 76, 77, 83
Breeches 21, 24, 25, 26, 28, 29, 31, 32, 33, 35, 37, 43, 46, 47, 48, 53, 54, 55, 56, 57, 58, 59, 60, 72, 74, 75, 76, 77, 83, 88, 91, 92
Buckles 21, 26, 40, 43, 46, 47, 48, 50, 55, 57, 59, 72, 74, 75, 76, 78, 83, 91
Bullion 17. 19, 25, 28, 35, 43, 72, 87
Buttons 17, 19, 23, 24, 25, 26, 27, 28, 29, 30, 31, 32, 33, 34, 35, 36, 43, 46, 47, 48, 49, 53, 54, 55, 56, 57, 58, 59, 60, 72, 74, 75, 76, 77, 78, 83, 84, 87, 88, 92

Captains
British: 11, 12, 15, 24, 25, 26, 30, 32, 35, 39, 84, 85, 86, 87; French: 47, 48, 49, 50, 52, 53, 54, 57, 68, 69; Spanish: 74, 75
Coat 16, 21, 23, 24, 26, 27, 28, 30, 31, 32, 33, 35, 36, 37, 42, 46, 47, 48, 49, 50, 53, 54, 55, 56, 57, 60, 72, 74, 75, 77, 85, 88, 92
Cockade 9, 21, 25, 35, 36, 47, 48, 54, 57, 58, 59, 72, 75, 76, 78, 85, 94
Cocked hat 19, 21, 23, 25, 28, 29, 31, 32, 33, 35, 47, 54, 55, 72, 75, 76, 85, 94
Collar 16, 23, 24, 26, 27, 28, 30, 31, 32, 33, 34, 35, 37, 42, 43, 46, 47, 48, 49, 50, 53, 54, 55, 56, 57, 58, 59, 60, 65, 72, 74, 75, 76, 77, 85, 86, 87
Cravat 23, 28, 86
Cuffs 17, 24, 26, 28, 30, 31, 32, 33, 35, 37, 46, 47, 48, 49, 50, 53, 54, 55, 57, 58, 59, 60, 72, 74, 75, 76, 77, 87
Cloak 54, 56, 59, 60, 85

Epaulette 7, 9, 16, 17, 22, 23, 25, 26, 31, 36, 46, 47, 49, 50, 52, 57, 58, 86, 87

Fringe 17, 19, 46, 47, 50, 52, 55, 57, 60, 86, 87, 91
Full Dress
British: 23, 24, 26, 27, 28, 29, 31, 35, 37, 38, 87; French: 42, 46, 47, 49, 50, 53, 55, 56, 59; Spanish: 72, 74, 75, 77, 78

Gaiters 35, 37, 38, 65, 76, 83
Gloves 15, 87
Gorget 36, 52, 87

Hat 19, 25, 33, 34, 35, 36, 47, 48, 50, 54, 55, 57, 58, 59, 75, 76, 77, 78, 94
Hessian boots 26, 29, 88

Jacket 9, 34, 35, 46, 48, 53, 55, 57, 59, 60, 76, 77, 78, 83, 86, 88, 92

Lace 16, 17, 19, 23, 24, 25, 26, 28, 31, 34, 35, 47, 48, 57, 59, 60, 72, 74, 75, 77, 78, 83, 85, 86, 87, 88, 91, 92
Lapels 16, 17, 22, 24, 26, 27, 28, 31, 32, 33, 36, 42, 47, 49, 50, 72, 74, 75, 76, 77, 84, 88, 92
Laurel leaf 19, 35, 68, 69, 71
Lieutenants
British: 11, 12, 21, 27, 28, 31, 35, 39, 71, 88, 92; French: 10, 49, 50, 52, 56, 57

Marines
British: 15, 17, 35, 36, 37, 89, 91; French: 9, 66, 67, 89; Spanish: 77
Midshipman
British: 12, 30, 39, 88, 89; French: 10, 49, 50, 52, 57, 60; Spanish: 75, 76, 82

Paymaster 89
Pelisse 7
Phyrigian cap 9
Physician 31, 39
Pigtail 9, 11, 34, 65, 91
Plume 7, 35, 36, 47, 52, 57, 72, 74, 75, 76, 77, 87
Pockets 17, 23, 26, 29, 32, 33, 35, 43, 46, 47, 48, 49, 50, 53, 54, 55, 56, 57, 58, 59, 60, 74, 92, 94
Purser 13, 34, 35

Queue 9, 91

Russia braid 31, 91

Sash 35, 46, 57, 72, 78, 91
Shirt 9, 34, 35, 65, 78, 87
Shoes 21, 26, 28, 43, 46, 55, 59, 65, 72, 74, 75, 76, 77, 78, 83, 91
Sleeves 23, 24, 43, 47, 49, 56, 88, 94
Straw hat 33, 78, 91
Surgeon 31, 39, 92
Stocking 21, 25, 26, 28, 29, 43, 65, 72, 74, 75, 76, 77, 78, 83, 88, 91, 92
Swords 24, 26, 28, 29, 35, 38, 39, 40, 47, 55, 57, 58, 59, 62, 68, 69, 71, 75, 76, 77, 78, 79, 94
Sword belt 26, 28, 31, 40, 41, 47, 50, 55, 57, 59, 72, 75, 91
Sword knot 41, 50, 55, 57, 58, 60, 91, 94

Trousers 9, 34, 35, 37, 38, 46, 53, 59, 77, 78, 91, 92

Undress
British: 21, 23, 24, 26, 28, 32, 36, 92, 94; French: 42, 46, 47, 48, 50, 54, 55, 56, 57, 59, 60; Spanish: 72, 75, 76, 77

Waistcoats 19, 21, 24, 25, 26, 27, 28, 29, 31, 32, 33, 35, 43, 46, 47, 49, 53, 55, 57, 58, 60, 72, 74, 75, 76, 77, 78, 91, 92
Warrant officers 31, 32, 39, 92